FLASH
JEWELRY MAKING
AND REPAIR
TECHNIQUES

By Therese Spears

Promenade Publishing

Photography by Michael Spears
Illustrations by Therese Spears
Printed in the United States of America

ISBN 0-932255-03-5

For information address:
        Promenade Publishing
        PO Box 2092
        Boulder, CO 80306
        A division of Promenade Enterprises, Inc.

CONTENTS

FINDINGS

BEAD STRINGING MATERIALS

BASIC STRINGING TECHNIQUES

PEARL KNOTTING

TREASURE NECKLACES AND MULTIPLE STRANDS OF BEADS USING CONES

SIMPLE EARRINGS AND PENDANTS

The easiest jewelry making technique is that of stacking beads on a headpin or eye pin. This is the best technique for the beginning jewelry maker because it is not complicated and does not require any skill. It only takes seconds to place the beads on the pin, and a moment to decide if the design is pleasing. Multiple beaded pins can be made then combined for more elaborate jewelry pieces when attached to a jump ring.

HEAD PINS

Head pins are like a straight pin without a point on the tip. Popular sizes to work with are 1" to 3" in length.

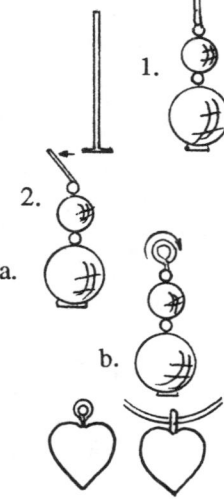

1. Any combination of shapes and sizes of beads can be used. Stack the beads on the pin.
2. Make a loop at the top. Cut the top of the wire off approximately 3/8" away from the top of the bead.
    a. Grasp the tip of the head pin with a roundnose plier. Depending on where the tip of the pin is placed in the plier will determine the size of the loop formed. Smaller loops are formed close to the tip of the plier. Bend the wire towards you forming a 45° angle.
    b. Firmly hold the plier and roll the wire away from you forming a perfect circle. This is best accomplished by rolling the wire with one continuous, sweeping motion of the hand.

The loop that now exists is used to attach to an ear finding (to be used as an earring), or some other type of finding suitable for its purpose.

This technique can also be used to make pendants out of beads that have a top to bottom hole. Be sure to take into consideration the direction the loop should face for correct placement.

Side-to-side for a dangle that will face front.

Front to back for a dangle that will be strung.

EYE PINS

Eye pins are used in the same manner as head pins in that beads are stacked onto the wire and a loop is formed at the top for attaching. The loop at the bottom of the eye pin is used to attach an ornament that will have movement and dangle.

1. Open the eye of the pin by bending the eye to the side with needlenose pliers or tweezers.
2. Thread on the item that will be hanging off of it. It can be a charm, pendant, or any object with a loop on the top of it.
3. Close the eye of the wire.
4. Stack any combination of beads onto the wire then make a loop at the top as described for Head Pins.

BAILS

A bail is used to make a pendant or dangle out of an ornament that has a side-to-side hole; or no hole at all with flat sides. Bails come in many shapes and sizes. Some have prongs that are pushed into the holes of the ornaments, and some have flat sides that are used for gluing. Both styles serve the same purpose — to enable the ornament to be strung or hung.

A.   B.   Front Views   A.   B.   Side Views   In Use

A bail with prongs is squeezed closed after the prongs have been inserted into the holes. Sometimes the prongs are at an angle and must be straightened out so they are level with the hole in the object. If they are not level ($\wedge$) the prongs may crack the glass ornament they are put into (especially Austrian crystal teardrops).

The flat bail is used by gluing it onto the ornament. Epoxy or jeweler's cement work best. The glue is placed on the insides of the bail and then closed around it.

Both styles of bails are available with or without a ring at the top. Take into consideration which direction the object is to be strung or hung.

Jewelry commonly incorporating bails are necklace pendants and dangles on earrings. Other uses are window hangings, mobiles and wind chimes made of flat slices of stone.

JUMP RINGS

Jump rings are generally an O-shaped ring that is available in a vast array of sizes. There are also oval and triangular shapes. The purpose of a jump ring is to connect one object to another. Jump rings can be connected to one another to form small chains. A single jump ring can change the direction a pendant or earring will hang. Also a single jump ring can form a pendant in the same manner as a bail.

A jump ring can attach a charm to an ear wire or post to form an earring that dangles, or has movement - - as opposed to merely hanging.

To use a jump ring properly, care must be taken to maintain its perfect shape. The jump ring must be opened correctly. Firmly grasp one end of the jump ring with a flatnose plier and push it to the side in the same manner an eye pin would be opened. A common mistake opening jump rings is by pulling it open like a jaw. The problem that arises is when the jump ring is closed it becomes mis-shaped.

SPLIT RINGS

A split ring is a double jump ring. The wire that forms the ring is wound around twice like a miniature key ring. It is more durable than a jump ring in that the item on it cannot be pulled off. A jump ring can open if stress is applied to it.

An article is placed in a split ring by first separating the ring at the tip, then threading the item around the ring until it is in the center.

Split rings are recommended for charms and clasp ends of heavy necklaces.

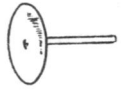

PAD POSTS

An easy, convenient way to convert clip earrings to pierced, or attach a post to a flat surface, is by using a pad post. The most common sizes are 4mm (3/32"), 8mm (5/16") and 10mm (5/8").

The surface of the article that the post will be adhered to must be free of oil or dirt (particularly in the case of vintage earrings). Use sand paper or a file to make the surface flat where the pad post will be placed. This will also roughen the area making a better bonding surface. Roughen the pad of the post. Use epoxy to glue the pad post to the back of the earring.

BAR PIN BACKS

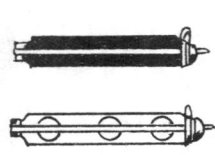

Pin backs come in a variety of sizes and styles. The average sizes range from 3/4" to 3". They are composed of a pin and a solid base made of metal or plastic. The base may have one, two or three holes punched in it. It may also be solid.

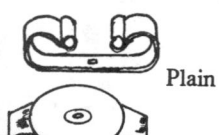

Gluing with epoxy is the best bonding technique. Roughen the surface to be bonded with sandpaper. Place the glue on the bar pin and stick it onto the ornament. If a pin back with holes is used, gently place it on the ornament so the epoxy flows through the holes to form small "buttons" on the top of it. This insures greater stability.

There are also bar pins that have a very strong adhesive tape on the back of the base. These are used by first pulling off the protective strip then sticking the base onto the object.

BOLO TIES

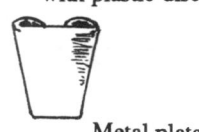

Plain

Bolo ties consist of four major parts: the bolo cord, bolo cord tips, bolo slide, and the decorative article.

There is a variety of bolo slides from which to choose. What they all have in common are two channels on the back in which each end of the bolo cord is strung. The possibilities of items that can be adhered onto the slides are limitless. Generally, the decorative piece is glued on with epoxy. To insure the best adhesion of non-porous pieces roughen the bolo slide and ornament surface to be bonded with sand paper.

with plastic disc

Metal plate

Bolo cords are made of woven leather, vinyl (leatherette), rayon/cotton blends (suedette, which has a suede or velvet-like appearance), and various other nylon and vinyl blends that give the appearance of metallic or matt cord. The average length is 36", however, bolo cords can be found in 42" lengths also.

Metal plate with clip

Bolo tips are made in two general styles. One has a smooth opening at the top for gluing in the bolo cord. The other has scalloped edges which can be pinched over the end of the bolo cord, therefore, crimping onto the bolo cord.

To make bolo:
1. Glue the decorative article onto the bolo slide
2. Thread each end of the bolo cord through the channels on the back
3. Attach the bolo tips to the cord ends.

CORD CRIMPS

Cord crimps are used to finish the ends of satin cord or leather lacing so that a clasp may be attached.

1.
2.
3.

1. Place one end of the cord into the crimp as shown.
2. Push one end of the crimp over the cord.
3. Fold the other end over to close the crimp.
4. Attach the clasp directly to the ring in the finding. If the clasp does not have a ring that can attach to the finding, use a jump ring.

CORD ENDS

Cord ends are hollow. Cover the end of the cord with glue or epoxy. Place the cord into the finding. If the cord is not snug, pieces of toothpicks can be inserted then broken off to fill the space.

Cord ends are available in various sizes so multiple strands of cord can be fit into one end.

METAL ORNAMENTS WITH HOLES FOR HANGING

There are decorative stamped metal ornaments that have multiple holes stamped out on the bottom of them to which eye pins, head pins, charms, strands of beads, and dangles of any type can be attached. These ornaments also have a hole or ring at the top to which ear wires, posts, clips, jump rings, or more beads can be attached.

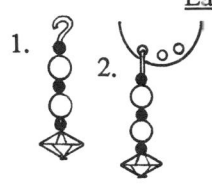

Earrings: Position beads on head pins or eye pins.

1. Form a loop at the top of the pin in the same manner as described under Head Pins, but do not close the loop completely.
2. Place the loop of the pin through the first hole of the decorative piece. Close it with flatnose pliers. Continue adding on the pins.

Brooches: Broaches are made in the same manner described above for the dangles. A pin back is glued to the back of the piece with epoxy.

A bead can be strung through the top hole of the piece, therefore hiding it.

Pendants: The beads are strung onto pins and attached in the same manner as for earrings. A jump ring is attached to the top hole. The pendant can then be strung.

SCREW EYES

This finding can be used to make a pendant or dangle from an ornament that has a small hole at the top of it, or is half drilled. They are available with varying lengths of screw ends, and also come in different sizes.

To use this finding merely coat the screw eye with epoxy or jeweler's cement and insert it into the opening. Be sure to place the eye in the correct position for its use.

BEAD STRINGING MATERIALS

Designing strung jewelry is a fun and rewarding experience. There are so many components available today. Design themes can range from ethnic, classical, simple and whimsical to name a few.

BEAD BOARDS

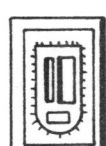

A helpful aid in designing is a bead board. It is a flat piece of plastic or wood with groves on which beads can be placed. They are made in different shapes and sizes. Most wooden boards are rectangular and range in size from 18" to 36". The best plastic ones have a U-shaped channel that has inch marks labeled on them. The center point is 0. The inch marks increase up each side, therefore making a piece an exact length is easy. Most of these boards have storage areas in them for the beads that you are working with. Placing a towel on the table will keep beads from rolling and also will keep dropped beads from bounding away. Although not as sophisticated as using a bead board, it also can be used to line up beads and design on.

NYMO®

This thread is a Belding Corticelli product that is used for stringing the small European glass seed beads. It is more durable than cotton or cotton/polyester blends.

BEAD CORD

This stringing material is made of silk or nylon. It is available on cards that are approximately 76" in length with a wire stringing needle woven into one end. It also comes on spools. There are many colors and sizes from which to choose.

Size 1 is the thinnest and works well for small beads such as fresh water pearls and 2mm beads with small holes. As the bead cord number increases the cord is thicker. Size 3 is an average size and can be used to string 4mm, 5mm and 6mm beads, depending on the size of the hole and the material of which they are made.

Also the weight of the beads will be a factor to take into consideration. A thin cord cannot support the weight of heavy beads.

Bead cord sizes increase up to size 12. Take a sample of the beads that are going to be strung with you when you purchase beading cord to be sure the correct size is chosen for the type of stringing techniques that will be used.

Generally silk bead cord makes more visually appealing knots than the nylon because of its sheen. It is also called Pearl Threading Silk.

Nylon is noted for its durability.

Bead cord should be stretched before using. Nylon usually has more "give" in it than silk. Take the bead cord off of the card. Starting at the end without the needle, hold approximately 12" of cord between your hands and pull. Do not let the cord slide through your hands or it could cut or burn the skin. Stretch the entire length of thread three times to insure the give is out of it.

To get any initial give out of the cord the beads can be strung without finishing the ends. Let the piece hang for a few days. Do not cut the needle off the cord. Once it is off, it cannot be used again because there isn't an eye that can be threaded.

The German brands of bead cord are the best quality.

The wire needle on the bead cord can acts as a file if a bead has a hole that is a bit too small. Place the bead on the needle then rub it back and forth to "file" the inside of the hole.

TIGERTAIL

Tigertail is nylon-coated steel cable that is extremely durable. It can be used for most beads, and is recommended especially for heavy ones. It is made in sizes for light, medium and heavy-weight beads. The size that is chosen depends on the weight of the beads of the entire piece of jewelry, the size of the holes in the beads, and the amount of stress or action the piece will receive. For example, a bracelet made of 4mm rose quartz beads will not have as much weight as a necklace made of 8mm hematite with metal charms. Therefore, a light weight tigertail is used for the bracelet, as opposed to a medium or heavy weight tigertail which will be used for the necklace.

Tigertail does not have the fluid movement of bead cord. It is a stiffer stringing material and less flexible.

The use of tigertail does not require a knot. A crimp bead is used instead of a knot when attaching the clasp. There are several styles and sizes:

They are made of metals such as brass, nickel, gold and silver plate, sterling silver, and gold plate over sterling.

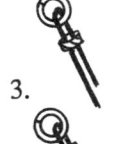

Stringing with tigertail:

Cut the desired length plus 2".

1. Pass the end of the tigertail through a crimp bead. Leave a 1/2" tail.

2. Pass the tail through one end of the clasp then back through the crimp bead.

3. Smash or crush the crimp bead with a pair of needlenose pliers. The object is to totally flatten the crimp.

The tail can be concealed by threading several beads over it. To do this with ease pick out 4 to 7 beads with the largest holes in them. These beads will be the first and last beads to be strung.

String the desired length of beads.

Crimp the opposite end in the same manner as described previously but thread the tigertail back through the beads before crushing the crimp. If there is excess tigertail that cannot be threaded through the beads it can be trimmed next to a bead.

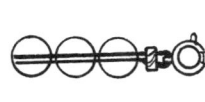

On occasion the beads may have very small holes so threading through them with the tails will be impossible. In that instance cut the tail of the tigertail off next to the crimp.

BASIC STRINGING TECHNIQUES

These techniques only vary in the way the clasp is attached. The main stringing technique is merely pushing the bead stringing needle through the bead then sliding it down next to the clasp or previous bead.

Use bead cord on a card as previously described for all of the following techniques.

A rapid way to restring beads that are temporarily strung or on a broken strand is to slide them off of the string in groups of three or more. Hold the beads stationary, keeping the holes in a line. Thread through the beads with a single motion.

If the beads to be restrung have large holes and are temporarily strung, taking the beads off of the strand and holding them is not necessary. Slide a group of beads down close to the end of the strand. String through them with the stringing needle. Slide the beads down the length of the bead cord.

* * * * *

Before basic stringing begins a clasp must first be attached. There are many ways to do this and several findings to choose from.

ATTACHING A CLASP USING KNOT COVERS OR KNOT TIPS

KNOT COVERS

This finding serves to hide and protect the knot. Generally they resemble and operate like a clam. When using this style do not use bead cord thicker than size 3.

Style A <u>Style A</u>. 1. Tie a knot in the end of the bead cord. Brush the knot with clear fingernail polish. Trim the tail of the cord close to the knot.

2.  2. Thread the bead cord through the hole in the center of the finding. The knot will rest in between the two shells.

Close the finding (in the same manner a clam would shut) with needlenose or roundnose pliers.

3.  3. Attach one end of the clasp by opening the ring on the end of the knot cover. Slip the clasp through the ring. Close the ring.

4. String the beads.

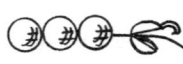 TO FINISH: String the knot cover onto the bead cord as shown. Slide it down next to the bead. Tie a loose single knot in the bead cord. Slide the knot down into the finding with a T-pin or beading awl.

Brush the knot with clear fingernail polish. Trim the bead cord close to the knot.
Attach the clasp.

 Style B

Style B. 1. Tie a knot in the end of the bead cord. Brush it with clear fingernail polish. Trim the tail of the cord close to the knot.

2. Place the knot into one of the shell halves. Be sure the bead cord is centered in the groove on the end of the shell. When the finding is squeezed together this groove becomes the hole that the bead cord comes through. If the cord is not centered in the groove it will be severed when the finding is closed.

3. Close the finding (in the same manner a clam would shut) with needlenose pliers.

4. Attach one end of the clasp by opening the ring on the end of the knot cover. Slip the clasp through the ring. Close the ring.

5. String the beads.

TO FINISH: Tie a loose single knot in the bead cord. Slide the knot down next to the last bead. Brush the knot with clear fingernail polish. Place the knot into one half of the shell of the finding. Center the bead cord over the groove. Close the finding. Trim the cord next to the finding.

Attach the other end of the clasp.

KNOT TIPS

Knot tips are used in the same relative manner as knot covers in that the knot is resting in a finding.

Single Strand Method

1. Tie a knot in the end of the bead cord. Brush it with clear fingernail polish. Trim the tail close to the knot.

2. Thread the bead cord through the knot tip so the knot will be resting inside of the cup.

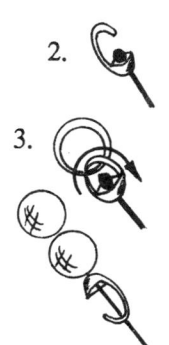

3. Place one half of the clasp on the open rung. Close the rung by rolling it shut with needlenose pliers. Be sure to maintain a nice shape.

4. String the beads.

TO FINISH: Thread through the knot tip as shown. Tie a loose single knot in the bead cord. Slide the knot down into the finding with a T-pin or beading awl. Brush the knot with clear fingernail polish. Trim the bead cord close to the knot.

Attach the clasp.

Double Strand Method

Use a double strand of bead cord threaded through a twisted wire beading needle.

1. Tie a single knot with two tails of the bead cord. Brush the knot with clear fingernail polish. Trim the tails of the cord off close to the knot.
2. Thread the bead cord through the hole in the knot tip so the knot is resting in the cup of the finding.

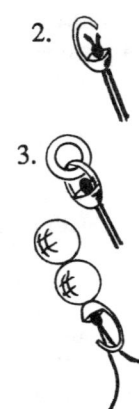

3. Place one end of the clasp on the open rung. Close the rung by rolling it shut with needlenose or roundnose pliers. Be sure to maintain a nice shape.
4. String the beads.

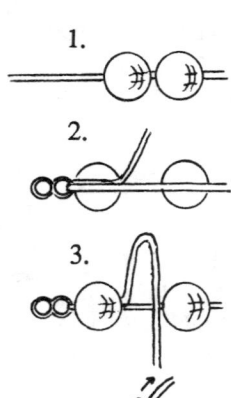

TO FINISH: Thread through the bead tip as shown. Cut the bead cord 2" to 3" away from the knot tip. Tie a square knot into the cup of the finding. A square knot is the same type of knot used to tie string around a mailing package or to join two pieces of rope together.

Place the right strand over and around the left strand. Pull the ends of the bead cord so the knot will slide down the length of thread into the cup of the finding. Place a T-pin or beading awl next to the knot so it will not travel.

Tie the second half of the square knot by placing the left strand over and around the right strand. Pull the knot down to rest on top of the previous knot. Remove the T-pin or awl. Pull the two cords a bit more so the knot is snug. Brush the knot with clear fingernail polish. Trim the attached ends close to the knot.

Attach the clasp.

TYING ON A CLASP

Select 4 beads that have large holes from the beads to be strung. These will be the first two and the last two beads.

1. String through 2 beads then slide them down to the end of the bead cord leaving a 1" tail.
2. String through the clasp then back through the first bead.
3. Tie a double overhand knot. This is done by making a loop with the bead cord as shown. Pass the needle and cord under the bead cord and then through the loop.
4. Pass the needle and cord through the loop again to form a double knot. Pull the bead cord and the knot will be formed

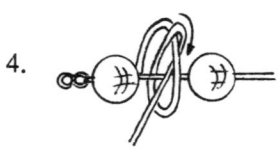

5.

next to the bead. Brush the knot with clear fingernail polish.

5. Pass the needle and cord through the second bead. Trim the tail of the cord off next to the bead.

6. String the beads. Rembember that the last two beads strung will be the ones with large holes.

TO FINISH: String through the clasp then back through the last bead. Make a double overhand knot. Brush the knot with clear fingernail polish. Pass the needle and cord through the second to the last bead. Cut the cord next to the bead.

BULLION OR FRENCH WIRE

This material is a tightly wound coil made of thin gold or silver plate wire. Using the coil gives a more professional finish to a necklace or bracelet. It is also extremely practical in that the coil makes the bead cord that is threaded around the clasp more durable. It is protected against fraying. The amount of coil used depends on the distance from the bead; through the end of the clasp; then back to the bead. Generally 1/4" to 3/8" is a good length.

Carefully cut the coil. It can be flattened or crushed easily. Be sure not to let the end catch on anything as it can easily stretch out.

1.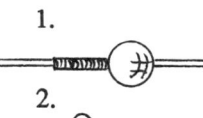

1. String the coil onto the bead cord and slide it down next to the bead.

2.

2. String the clasp onto the bead cord then over the coil.

3.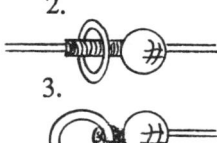

3. String the bead cord back through the bead. The coil will form a casing around the bead cord on which the clasp rests.

4. Proceed with the stringing or knotting technique.

PEARL KNOTTING

SINGLE STRAND PEARL KNOTTING
Before the actual stringing and knotting begins, one half of the clasp must be attached to the bead cord using one of the techniques described in the previous chapter.

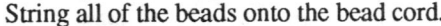

String all of the beads onto the bead cord.
Slide a bead next to the knot cover or knot tip.
If the clasp is attached without the use of a knot cover or tip begin knotting after the second bead.

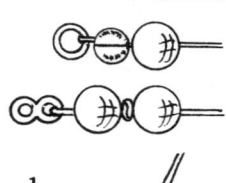

KNOTTING
1.
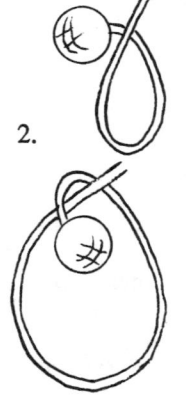
2.
1. Tie a single knot by making a loop in the bead cord as shown.
2. Put the bead and clasp through the loop. This forms a very loose knot with a large loop.
3. Using a T-pin (available at most fabric stores) or beading awl, slide the knot down next to the bead. Pull the bead cord tight to form the knot around the T-pin or awl. Give the knot a push with your thumb or index fingernail to be sure the knot is as close to the bead as it can get. Do not get discouraged if the first knot you tie does not rest exactly next to the bead. The more you do it the better you get. It is best to do a practice piece first before starting an expensive project.

Generally, it is easier for right-handed people to slide the knots down working from left to right. The knotted beads will be laying on the right side of the bead cord.

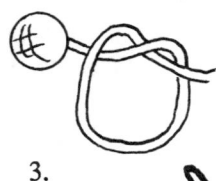

To knot rapidly use this variation of the technique. After the loop of bead cord has been formed place the T-pin or awl through the loop next to the bead. Pull the bead cord tight forming the knot. This is also how knotting tweezers are used. The tweezers are placed onto the cord through the loop next to the bead. When the cord is pulled the knot forms around the tips of the tweezers, then slides down next to the bead. Remove the T-pin, awl or tweezers. Push the knot with your fingernail to insure it is next to the bead.

3.
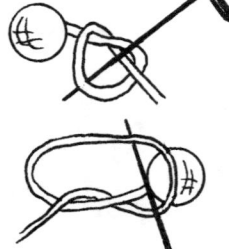

* * * * *

A trick for placing the knot as close to the bead as possible and knot rapidly is to position the knot close to the bead leaving the knot a bit loose. Hold onto the bead cord with one hand and with the other hand slide the next bead up to the knot and push the knot with the bead. The knot will be quickly placed next to the bead. This saves wear and tear on long fingernails!

TO FINISH
Finish the necklace off by attaching the opposite end of the clasp to the bead cord.

If the clasp is attached without knot cover or knot tip, do not pearl knot between the last two beads. The final knot is placed there after stringing on the clasp.

DOUBLE STRAND PEARL KNOTTING

USING KNOT COVERS TO ATTACH THE CLASP

Usually double strand knotting is not used with knot covers because the two strands of bead cord are too thick to fit in a knot cover. However, it will work with size 1 comfortably. The knots will be small.

1.

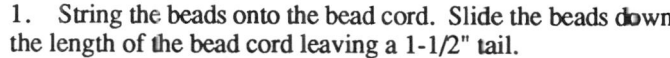

1. String the beads onto the bead cord. Slide the beads down the length of the bead cord leaving a 1-1/2" tail.
2. Measure the length of the strung beads. Divide that amount in half. Add 3" to that length. Cut the bead cord that distance away from the beads. Place a piece of tape on one end of the cut cord. This will keep the beads from sliding off.

3.

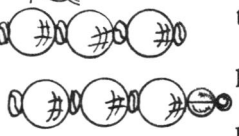

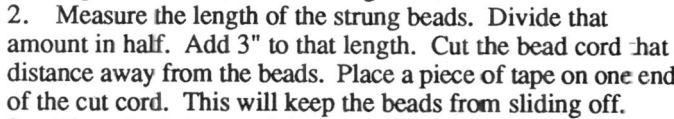

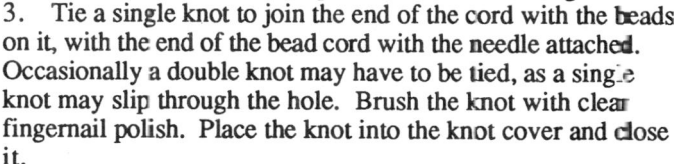

3. Tie a single knot to join the end of the cord with the beads on it, with the end of the bead cord with the needle attached. Occasionally a double knot may have to be tied, as a single knot may slip through the hole. Brush the knot with clear fingernail polish. Place the knot into the knot cover and close it.

String through the first bead and then begin the knotting technique.

To finish, tie the final knot. Brush it with clear fingernail polish. Close the knot cover around the knot.

The clasp ends can be attached after the piece is knotted, rather than attaching one half at a time.

USING KNOT TIPS TO ATTACH THE CLASP

1. Thread on the knot tip leaving a 1-1/2" tail. String all of the beads onto the bead cord and the other knot tip. Be sure the last tip is facing the opposite direction of the first one. Measure the length of the beads strung. Divide that amount in half. Add 3" to that length. Cut the bead cord that distance away from the beads. Place a piece of tape on the end of the cord.
2. Thread the remaining bead cord through the knot tip leaving a 1-1/2" tail. Tie the two tails together into a knot. Brush the knot with clear fingernail polish. Position the knot to rest in the cup.

String through the first bead then begin the knotting technique.

Finishing is done by tying the final square knot into the cup of the finding. Brush the knot with clear fingernail polish. Trim the ends of the cords next to the knots. Attach the clasp.

1.

2.

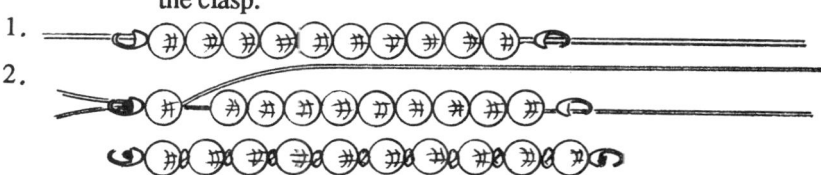

ATTACHING THE CLASP WITHOUT KNOT COVER OR TIP

1.   Pick out three beads with large holes to be the first and the last beads strung. String one of the beads and one half of the clasp onto the bead cord. Slide them down the length of the bead cord until they are 12" away from the end. String the needle and cord back through the bead. Place a piece of tape on the end of the cord.

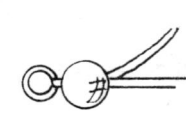

String the beads onto the bead cord with the first and last beads being the ones with large holes. String on the other end of the clasp. Slide the beads and clasp down one half the length of the bead cord. Most beginning knotters are comfortable positioning the beads at this spot for 18" to 26" necklaces, because that way the beginner can be confident there will be enough cord to complete the knotting. This position will change with experience.

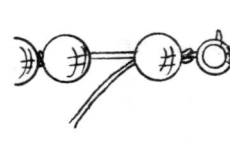

Thread the needle back through the last bead. This will secure the clasp.

DOUBLE STRAND PEARL KNOTTING TECHNIQUE

This technique produces a tighter knotted necklace than the single strand technique. It will not be as fluid. However, this technique is quicker to accomplish and the knots easily rest against the beads.

1.   Make a loop of cord over the bead cord that has the beads strung on it.

1.

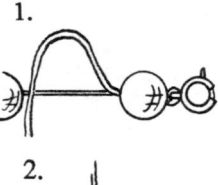

2.   Bring the bead cord needle and thread through the loop and pull to form the knot. The knot will tie itself right next to the bead.

2.

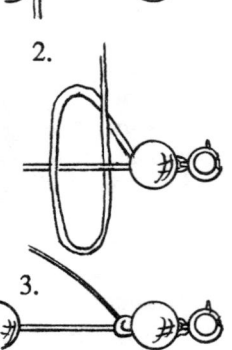

3.   String through the next bead and slide it down next to the knot.

Proceed with knotting.

TO FINISH: If a knot tip or knot cover was used, tie the two tails of thread together in a square knot then finish in accordance with that type of finding.

To finish without a knot cover or tip, do not make a knot between the last two beads remaining on the bead cord.

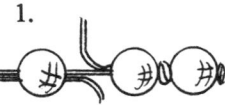

1. Slide the bead that is on the opposite end of the cord almost next to the unknotted bead. Leave enough room for a knot to be tied.

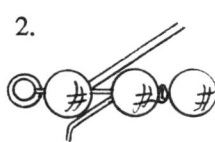

2. Ease the clasp down next to the bead by pulling on the bead cord that has the free end.

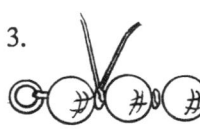

3. Bring one end of the bead cord around the cord that the beads are strung on and tie a square knot with the two strands. Brush the knot with clear fingernail polish.

If the holes in the beads are large enough, thread the tails of the bead cord through the beads to conceal them. The tail that has the needle on it should thread through easily. A fine, flexible twisted wire beading needle will have to be threaded onto the opposite tail in order to pass the cord through the bead.

Trim the cord next to the bead.

If a square knot was tied and the tails cannot be concealed, trim the tails close to the knot.

TREASURE NECKLACES AND MULTIPLE STRANDS OF BEADS USING CONES

Treasure necklaces are a blend of a multitude of beads. They originally were composed of mainly old trade beads with a Native American flair. Now they are being created with just about any material: glass, rare hangings, crystal, and semi-precious beads. Some of these necklaces "recycle" old jewelry. You can take apart old necklaces to use the beads, and add "treasures" from the jewelry box that haven't been seen for years - - such as rings, earrings and pendants. These necklaces can be an exploration of color themes. Working with hues of color, experimenting with color combinations and using various styles of beads can be fun and exciting.

MULTIPLE STRANDS USING CONES
Supplies needed:

| 2 or more strands of beads | 1 pair of cones |
| 1 clasp | 1 pair of eye pins |

This use of findings is for necklaces and bracelets that have multiple strands. Cones vary in length, width, style and metallic composition. Choose a pair that matches the metal in the jewelry piece or is aesthetically pleasing.

1.   String the strands of beads to the desired length, leaving a 1-1/2" to 2" tail on both sides of the beads. Tape one group of
1.   tails to the table.

STRUNG WITH BEAD CORD OR NYMO®

2.   To attach the eye pin, carefully divide the tails of the free end of strands into two groups. Tie a square knot close to the beads. Thread one group of strands through the eye pin. The strands may have to be licked to keep them together. Thread the other group through the eye pin in the opposite direction. Tie the two groups of thread into a square knot. Tie an additional half of a square knot for good luck. (You do not want this knot to come untied!) Glue the knot with jeweler's cement or any other non-water soluble glue.
3.   Thread the eye pin through the large opening of the cone up through the smaller hole. Pull the eye pin from the top until the knot at the bottom is no longer exposed and is secure in the cone.

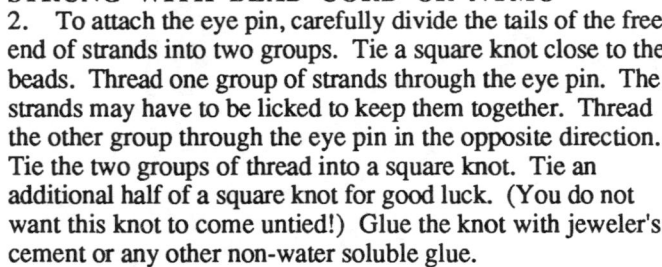

2.

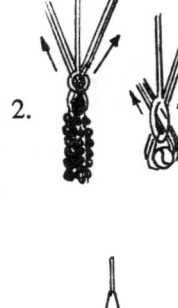

3.

4.   Cut the eye pin approximately 3/8" away from the top of the cone. Form a loop in the same manner as described for Head Pins. Bend the wire towards you, then roll it away in the opposite direction with a continuous motion. Do not completely close the loop. One end of the clasp must be threaded onto it. Close the loop after the clasp is in place.

5.   Tape down the finished end. Lift up the strands that were previously taped down. The beads will flow down next to the cone attached to the opposite end. A knot can be tied next to the beads to now insure their position, or the eye pin can now be attached. Finish this end by attaching the cone and clasp.

STRUNG WITH TIGERTAIL

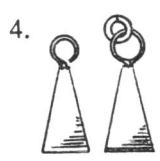

If the necklace being made will be heavy, an extra loop can be made in the eye pin with a roundnose plier. The double loop will serve as a split ring and guarantee the weight of the necklace will not pull open the eye pin.
1.   Attach one strand of beads at a time to each of the eye pin. String on the crimp. Pass the tigertail through eye pin and then back through the crimp. Crush the crimp. For a very heavy necklace, two crimps can be used as one, therefore insuring greater strength.

There must be a small amount of space between the eye pin and beads or the tigertail will be very rigid, therefore making the necklace stiff. Hold up the strand to gage where the crimp on the opposite end of the strand should be placed to have the piece flow.

Attach the tigertail to the eye pin in the same manner as described previously.

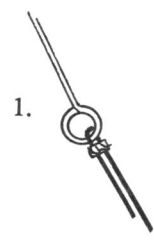

The remaining strands will be attached to the eye pins in the same manner.
2.   Thread the eye pin through the large opening of the cone up through the smaller end. Pull the eye pin from the top until the group of crimps are no longer visible. Sometimes the loop in the eye pin is too large to do this so it must be flattened a bit with needlenose pliers so that it may go farther up the cone.

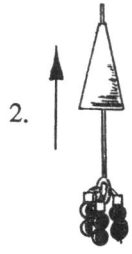

3.   Cut the pin approximately 3/8" away from the top of the cone. Form a loop in the same manner as described for Head Pins (bend the wire towards you, then roll it away in the opposite direction). Do not completely close the loop. One end of the clasp must be threaded onto it.

Close the loop after the clasp is in place.

OR

Do not cut the pin. Slide the clasp onto the wire. Bend the wire into a loop shape with round nose pliers. Wrap the excess wire around the base of the loop several times. Cut off the excess wire then press the tip down so it won't catch or scratch anything. This is recommended for heavy necklaces.

5. Place the opposite eye pin through the cone and finish the other side of the piece.

Other books by Promenade Publishing:

Beaded Clothing Techniques by Therese Spears   ISBN 0-93225-01-9

Contemporary Loomed Beadwork
by Therese Spears   ISBN 0-932255-02-7

Flash Jewelry Making Techniques
by Therese Spears   ISBN 0-932255-03-5

Beaded Dream Catchers
by Mary R. Musgrove   ISBN 0-932255-05-1

French Beaded Flowers I
by Helen McCall   ISBN 0-932255-04-3

HEARTS LIKE FISTS

FISTS

BY ADAM SZYMKOWICZ

★

★

DRAMATISTS
PLAY SERVICE
INC.

HEARTS LIKE FISTS
Copyright © 2013, Adam Szymkowicz

All Rights Reserved

SPECIAL NOTE

Originally commissioned by South Coast Repertory
with support from the Elizabeth George Foundation.

Originally produced by Theatre of NOTE, Hollywood, CA.

For my parents, whose support is immeasurable

ACKNOWLEDGMENTS

Special thanks in no particular order to Seth Glewen, South Coast Rep, Elizabeth George, Megan Monaghan, Polly Carl, Keith Powell, Joe Kraemer, Richard Feldman, Marsha Norman, Chris Durang, Jim Houghton, The Juilliard School, Evan Cabnet, Mimi O'Donnell, LAByrinth Theater, Stephen Willems, Mark Schultz, MCC Theater, Kristen Palmer, John and Rhoda Szymkowicz, Larry Kunofsky, Tish Dace, Kimberly Yates, Moxie Street Picture Shows, The Chance Theater, Oanh Nguyen, Jeremy Aluma, Holland Productions, Stacey Luftig, Devan Sipher, Christina Shipp, Jeret Ochi, all the amazing actors in the workshop at Juilliard or who were in the various readings, Mandi Moss, Jaime Robledo, Theater of Note, Emily Owens, Kelly O'Donnell, Gus Schulenburg, and Flux Theatre Ensemble.

HEARTS LIKE FISTS was first produced by Mandi Moss and Jason Moyer for Theatre of NOTE in Los Angeles, California, opening on August 3, 2012. It was directed by Jaime Robledo; the set design was by DeAnne Millais; the costume design was by Takashi Morimoto; the lighting design was by Matt Richter; the sound design was by Mark McClain Wilson; the fight choreography was by Andrew Amani; and the stage manager was Bebe Herrera. The cast was as follows:

LISA .... Lauren Dobbins Webb
PETER .... Rick Steadman
DOCTOR X .... Keith Allan
NINA .... Alysha Brady
SALLY .... Jennifer Lee Weaver
JAZMIN .... Alina Phelan
NURSE .... Grace Eboigbe
STAGE NINJA 1 .... Dan Wingard
STAGE NINJA 2 .... Pierce Baird

HEARTS LIKE FISTS was subsequently produced by Flux Theatre Ensemble in New York City at the Secret Theatre, opening on December 1, 2012. It was directed by Kelly O'Donnell; the set design was by Will Lowry; the costume design was by Stephanie Levin; the lighting design was by Kia Rogers; the sound design was by Janie Bullard; the fight choreography was by Adam Swiderski; and the production stage manager was Jodi M. Witherell. The cast was as follows:

LISA .... Marnie Schulenburg
PETER .... Chinaza Uche
DOCTOR X .... August Schulenburg
NINA .... Becky Byers
SALLY .... Aja Houston
JAZMIN .... Rachael Hip-Flores
NURSE .... Susan Louise O'Connor
THE COMMISSIONER .... Chris Wight
ENSEMBLE .... Jennifer Somers Kipley, Chester Poon

CHARACTERS

LISA, a crimestopper, female

PETER, a heart doctor, male

DOCTOR X, evil but misunderstood, male

NINA, a Crimefighter, female

SALLY, a Crimefighter, female

JAZMIN, a Crimefighter, female

NURSE, a nurse, female

THE COMMISSIONER, played by the actor who plays Doctor X

MAN, played by the actor who plays Peter

WOMAN, played by the actor who plays Nurse

GIRL, played by the actor who plays Jazmin

CARSON, played by the actor who plays Doctor X

ED, played by the actor who plays Peter

Note: Actors can be any race.

PLACE

New York City.

TIME

Now.

HEARTS LIKE FISTS

Prologue

Spotlight on Doctor X, a truly terrible creature with sunken eyes and deep scars all over. Disfigured, stethoscope around the neck, wearing a doctor's lab coat, carrying a doctor's bag.

DOCTOR X.   I have a face like a bowl of worms. Squirming around the ticks, the scars, the moles. It's disgusting. A face like this. It's absurd, without meaning or purpose. And I honestly can't say if I'm an experiment gone awry or if I was just born this way. I have no origin. I have no memory. I can only remember you. The way you looked at me, the first time you saw me, it was like you saw the bowl underneath the worms. Your face was like a china plate. Perfect. Whole. Pristine. And you looked at me, the way you looked at me — The patient had died. That much I remember. His wife was wailing but I couldn't hear her. Because you were there and everything else melted away. "Let's have a drink," you said with your face like a plate. And we drank and we drank and we went to my place and we made love like normal people. And it continued that way for days, weeks, years. I can't say for sure. Why can't I remember? If I could only remember, maybe I could find you. Or maybe I could figure out when how why you grew tired of me. Was it then I became what I am? Your body was like liquor and I couldn't get enough, couldn't spend a night without you, a minute, a second. I didn't know you weren't drunk on me. How could I have missed the diagnosis? How could I have avoided the bald shock, the morning discovery, to wake up and find your note? And now I can't remember anything except you. Your face everywhere I go. You will pay. Everyone will pay. You will all pay dearly.

1

The three Crimefighters on stage. They are dressed right out of a comic book with masks over their eyes. They are fierce. Flashbulbs may go off. Jazmin and Nina may pose for the cameras in various positions. Sally does not.

SALLY. Thank you all for coming. I'm sure you know who we are.

NINA. You've seen us on the news.

JAZMIN. Perhaps you have a poster on your wall.

SALLY. Or a story you tell over and over about the time you brushed Nina's sleeve.

NINA. Or when Sally saved your cousin from a burning building.

SALLY. Or when your brother had a date with Jazmin.

JAZMIN. He just wasn't my type.

NINA. But that's not why you're here. Just to gape at us.

JAZMIN. Maybe they're here a little because of that.

SALLY. You want to hear if anything is being done.

NINA. About the murders.

JAZMIN. The senseless murders that happen almost every night.

SALLY. Let me assure you we are working on it.

JAZMIN. We are close to solving it.

NINA. We know who is doing it.

SALLY. We're just waiting to catch the Doctor.

NINA. We're near to finding Doctor X's lair.

JAZMIN. He's been a hard nut to crack.

SALLY. We've almost rid the city of crime.

NINA. Because of us, Clownface, the Electric Eel and the Red Witch are behind bars.

SALLY. And don't forget Fire Storm, Don Oregon, the Gambler, the Head, the Economist, the Dentist, Johnny Steel and Little Orphan Drillnose —

JAZMIN. All in jail. And Muddlehead, the Monkey Twins, the Leather Fist, Volcano Moe, the Annihilator, the Incubator, Tarantula Sue, Lulu the Circus Freak and Millionaire Ted —

NINA. All presumed dead. Because of our hard work and dedication.

SALLY. But Doctor X eludes us still. *(A static sound like from a walkie-talkie.)*

COMMISSIONER. Crimefighters!

SALLY, JAZMIN, NINA. Commissioner. *(Light up on the Commissioner, but perhaps we see only part of the commissioner or his back is to us or he wears a hat low to hide his face. The Commissioner is a mystery.)*

COMMISSIONER. It happened again last night.

SALLY, JAZMIN, NINA. No!

COMMISSIONER. On Forty-Third Street.

SALLY. Was it the same as the others?

COMMISSIONER. The same.

SALLY. Shoot!

JAZMIN. Snap!

NINA. Darn! *(Sally, Nina and Jazmin walk into the crime scene. There is yellow crime-scene tape surrounding a bed. A man and a woman, dead, lie entwined in each other's arms. Note: can be dummies in the bed.)*

JAZMIN. Just like the others.

NINA. Two lovers, dead, their hearts stopped by a poison that attacks the heart.

SALLY. They were asleep when they died.

JAZMIN. Entwined in each other's arms. The sleep of lovers.

NINA. Now the death of lovers.

SALLY. It was Doctor X.

JAZMIN. No doubt. *(The lights change and the three step out of the bedroom area. The man and woman are alive now, asleep. Perhaps light snoring.)*

SALLY. Doctor X came in through the window, up from the fire escape. *(Enter Doctor X, dressed the same as at the top of the play, carrying a doctor's bag.)*

DOCTOR X. Look at them, lying there. I can't look at them Oh, look at them. I can't look at them. Lying there, in each other's arms. *(Shouting.)* No one will ever hold me like that! *(The man stirs but does not wake.)* Shhh! There there now. Sleep sleep. *(The man begins to snore again. Taking two hypodermics from the doctor's bag.)* You're going to sleep for a long long time. *(Doctor X injects them both. Their hearts stop.)*

NINA. There was someone else there.

JAZMIN. Last night? *(Lisa enters the same way Doctor X did.)*

LISA. Stop that. You! Stop! *(Doctor X turns. Lisa attacks him.)*

9

NINA. There was a struggle. *(Doctor X and Lisa struggle. A fight which goes on for a little while. The Crimefighters narrate their fight and Doctor X and Lisa perform the actions described.)*
JAZMIN. He jabs once, twice, left, then right.
SALLY. But she ducks.
NINA. She hits him with a right hook.
SALLY. He counters with a jab to the ribs.
NINA. It hurts but she doesn't fall.
JAZMIN. She swings wildly.
SALLY. But she misses.
JAZMIN. And he shoves her.
NINA. And then she trips and falls here.
SALLY. He jumps at her but she rolls out of the way.
NINA. She kicks him from the ground.
SALLY. Hits his knee hard.
JAZMIN. But he gets back up.
SALLY. He grabs her.
JAZMIN. He tries to strangle her
SALLY. She knees him in the groin.
NINA. A somersault. Two somersaults.
JAZMIN. He's on top of her.
SALLY. She karate-chops his leg.
NINA. He punches her in the head, hard.
JAZMIN. She lies there, a little dazed.
NINA. A little hurt.
SALLY. Disappointed.
JAZMIN. While he makes his escape. *(Doctor X escapes, limping.)*
NINA. *(Examining the syringe she picks up off the ground.)* Sometime during the tussle, she got scratched by the syringe. *(Lisa looks at the scratch on her arm.)*
SALLY. She's mad at herself for letting him escape.
NINA. She got there too late to save the lovers.
JAZMIN. But she could have stopped him from leaving.
SALLY. Or she thought she could have.
NINA. Couldn't she have?
SALLY. She sat there.
NINA. Did she cry?
SALLY. She may have cried.
JAZMIN. And then she left.
SALLY. She left.

NINA. She left. *(Exit Lisa.)*
JAZMIN. Where did she go?
SALLY. We need to find her.
NINA. But where should we look?
JAZMIN. The trail is cold.
SALLY. We're going to be late for work.

2

A hospital. The Crimefighters take off their masks and become nurses. They are joined by Nurse. Lisa in another area being examined by Peter, a heart doctor.

LISA. Thank you for seeing me so soon.
PETER. It's no problem.
SALLY. She came.
JAZMIN. Is it her?
NINA. It might be.
NURSE. Who?
SALLY. No one. A girl.
JAZMIN. Is she in there?
NINA. She's in there with him.
NURSE. Lucky girl.
LISA. It's comforting to be taken care of so quickly. It's very kind of you.
PETER. Please. It's my job.
LISA. I'm sure you must be very busy these days, what with the rash of heart crimes.
PETER. Lots of people worried about their hearts. Lots of people sleeping alone. People who don't even have to sleep alone. Don't even want to. Lots of fear.
LISA. I was scratched.
PETER. You were?
LISA. By a syringe.
PETER. So you're concerned.
LISA. I have concerns.

PETER. Well, let's take a listen.

NURSE. He listened to my heart once.

SALLY. He did?

NINA. He didn't. *(Lisa opens her shirt. Peter takes the stethoscope and listens to her heart.)*

JAZMIN. Was the stethoscope cold?

NURSE. Only a little.

NINA. Were his hands warm?

NURSE. He brushed my arm with his fingertips. They were like butterflies.

SALLY. Did you kiss him?

NURSE. I was too afraid. There was his breath in my ear. Pounding in my throat. I remember, he said —

PETER. Your heart is beating fast.

LISA. Is it?

PETER. You need to relax.

NURSE. He listened for a long time but when he was done, he told me I could go.

JAZMIN. And you went?

NURSE. There was nothing else to do.

PETER. *(To Lisa.)* You have a strong heart. There are other tests I can run if you want but from what I've heard your heart is strong and capable of many things.

LISA. Thank you. That's nice to hear.

PETER. Not everyone has such a strong heart. My own heart. It was damaged once and has never quite been able to recover. It's a muscle you know.

LISA. I know.

PETER. And it atrophies if you don't use it. Sometimes I don't use mine as much as I should. Yours, though. You can be as active as you want. A heart like that.

LISA. Thank you, Doctor.

PETER. Call me Peter.

LISA. Thank you, Peter. *(Pause.)* There's something else I wanted to ask you about.

PETER. Oh.

LISA. Sorry.

PETER. No. No. You heard about my experiments. It's hard to keep anything a secret. I tried to keep it out of the papers, but I guess in the current climate — People are afraid to sleep together even when they shut their windows and lock their doors. My artificial heart would of course protect them. We could all sleep with our lovers without fear. We wouldn't fear to love.

LISA. You have a lover you're afraid to love?

PETER. No, no. With this heart? No, not me.

LISA. There's not anyone?

PETER. No, not now. Not anymore. Not anyone.

LISA. But I'm sure, a man like you —

PETER. Please. I don't want to talk about it.

LISA. Sorry. I just thought —

PETER. You were asking about the artificial heart. I'm going to be the first test subject. I can't do the operation myself of course. But if the heart works on me and my body doesn't reject it …

LISA. But what if something happened to you while you were under the knife?

PETER. It's a risk I'm willing to take. For science.

LISA. Oh.

PETER. What is it?

LISA. My father died under the knife.

PETER. I see.

LISA. During surgery. So it scares me. You're brave.

PETER. No. Not at all.

LISA. You are.

PETER. Well, Okay.

LISA. And a brave man like you shouldn't be afraid of love. I mean, don't you want to?

PETER. Me? Oh, no. Not me.

LISA. Why not?

PETER. My heart can't handle it. *(Lisa kisses him. A sound of a heart beating fast can be heard.)*

LISA. It handled that Okay. *(Peter looks shocked.)*

NURSE. I could fall in love with that doctor.

JAZMIN. Me too.

NINA. In another life.

PETER. Well, I think we're done here. I have other patients. You, I'm sure have other —

LISA. Come out to dinner with me.

PETER. Well — I — I don't normally — with patients.

LISA. Have dinner with me.

PETER. It's not —

13

LISA. Come out to dinner.
PETER. Okay, Yes. Okay. Yes. I would love to join you for dinner.

3

A restaurant. Peter and Lisa having dinner.

LISA. And I saw someone climbing a fire escape. So what else could I do? I followed.
PETER. You were very brave.
LISA. Not at all. Anyone else would have done the same thing.
PETER. Oh, I don't know. *(Beat.)*
LISA. There is something I should tell you.
PETER. What is it?
LISA. I've broken a lot of hearts. Too many to count really. I don't mean to. It just sort of happens.
PETER. I see.
LISA. That's why I've been out of the game so long. Too many people got hurt.
PETER. I appreciate you telling me this. I think I knew already in a way. Something about how every man's eye was drawn to you when you walked in the door on my arm. A girl like that can do a lot of damage. And not even on purpose.
LISA. It's not on purpose.
PETER. When they saw you, I felt all their hearts stop for a second. They all skipped a beat. Something about your eyes or your lips or the way you walk. Something about your shoulder or your hair or the color of your skin. Something inside you, just below the surface: a musical, a roller coaster, a sledgehammer.
LISA. I used to work in construction, but too many men fell to their deaths.
PETER. What do you do now?
LISA. They pay me to stay away from all the construction sites in the city.
PETER. They pay you not to work?
LISA. It's not fulfilling.

14

PETER. How many people were hurt?

LISA. I remember the last one. *(Enter Girl. Lisa and Girl shift to perhaps a semi-different location.)*

GIRL. So that's it, then?

LISA. I'm sorry.

GIRL. Was it something I did?

LISA. Not really.

GIRL. Is it who I am?

LISA. No. I mean you are who you are and someone will love that more than anything. Perhaps already there have been those people who want nothing but you, but that person isn't me and it's not fair to you, not to mention that I just don't think I'm really into girls. I mean, not enough anyway. Not as much as guys and I'm glad I know that now but maybe you're not as glad to hear it. But it's the truth and I guess sometimes the truth is unfortunate. So I'm sorry.

GIRL. You're burning a hole through the center of me. I'm not sure I'll ever recover.

LISA. That's just how it feels now. It'll heal.

GIRL. You don't know that.

LISA. Everything always heals.

GIRL. Not this. You don't know. No one has ever left you.

LISA. I guess that's true.

GIRL. You're always the one to leave. I should have taken that as a warning. I'm so stupid.

LISA. You're not.

GIRL. I'm a great girl.

LISA. I know. I know. I'm sorry.

PETER. *(To Lisa.)* Oh. I see.

LISA. I've said too much.

PETER. No, it's just — I mean that's my story but in reverse. It's kind of painful to hear. *(Girl goes over to Peter's side.)*

GIRL. We can still be friends.

PETER. Sure. Fine.

GIRL. Don't be like that.

PETER. How should I be?

GIRL. I don't know. Okay, be like that.

PETER. Was it something I did?

GIRL. No, nothing like that.

PETER. I'm just not sufficient? For your needs I mean?

GIRL. That's one way to say it I guess. We just don't belong together. You can see that, can't you?

PETER. I can see you saying that.

GIRL. I've hurt you.

PETER. I'll recover.

GIRL. You will?

PETER. Of course. My heart is resilient. *(Exit Girl.)*

LISA. But it's not.

PETER. No, it's not.

LISA. Now I've scared you.

PETER. I'm just not sure I can go through it again. *(Lisa kisses him.)* Oh. But then there's that.

LISA. Yeah.

PETER. Which makes me forget. Like a ten-second amnesia. Like a goldfish.

LISA. I like you, Peter.

PETER. I like you, too.

LISA. I'm going to the ladies room. I hope you'll tell me about your artificial hearts when I return.

PETER. I'd be delighted.

4

Lisa exits to the bathroom. The Crimefighters descend upon her there. Peter remains well lit.

SALLY. Lisa.

LISA. Sally, Jazmin, Nina.

NINA. Yes.

JAZMIN. It is us.

LISA. The Crimefighters! But what are you doing here and how do you know my name?

SALLY. We have connections at hospitals.

JAZMIN. We looked for patients with recent puncture wounds who seemed especially interested in their hearts.

NINA. And we followed you.

LISA. I see.

SALLY. You're the only civilian who has ever tussled with Doctor X and lived to talk about it. Did you know that?

LISA. No. I didn't know.

SALLY. Well it's true.

NINA. You've shown a lot of bravery.

LISA. No.

JAZMIN. He left with a limp. You gave him that at least.

LISA. I guess. It's funny though.

SALLY. What?

NINA. What?

JAZMIN. What?

LISA. He didn't respond to me the way men usually respond. I'm not saying every man loses his balance when he looks at me, but most of them do.

NINA. Huh.

JAZMIN. That's interesting.

LISA. I mean, he's not gay, I don't think.

SALLY. This is a guess. But I know sometimes obsession prevents us from seeing what's really in front us.

NINA. Why are you looking at me?

SALLY. I'm not.

JAZMIN. She's not.

LISA. Anyway, it was nice to meet you. I got checked out by a doctor, so I'm okay.

SALLY. On behalf of the city, on behalf of humanity. Thank you for fighting.

LISA. I just did what anyone else would have done.

SALLY. Not anyone. Most people don't rush in to danger. Most people slink away. Very few people scale fire escapes in order to engage mastermind criminals in hand to hand combat.

LISA. Okay, I mean I guess I see your point.

SALLY. You're a very impressive woman.

LISA. Thank you.

JAZMIN. Very courageous.

SALLY. Just like I said, isn't she?

NINA. Maybe more so.

JAZMIN. You think?

SALLY. Excuse us for a second. *(The Crimefighters huddle and whisper to one another. On the other side of the stage, Peter is wrestling internally.)*

PETER. She will hurt you. She will break you over her knee.

She will hurt you and she will tear you and she will rip you apart. Who are you that you think you can withstand her? You are just a man. You are a vulnerable man with tiny veins and blood rushing through you too fast. You have your career. You don't need complications. Not now. Now when the heart is just about ready to be tested. You are no one. No one and the heart is everything and you can't sacrifice these things for a tingling in your toes. For a pretty face. Such a pretty pretty face. Carries an electromagnetic field wherever she goes. Makes your heart beat faster than it has in years. She will break you. She will hurt you and tear you and break you and pull you until there will be nothing of you left. She will — *(Peter stands. He takes his coat and leaves the restaurant. The Crimefighters come out of their huddle.)*

SALLY. My father was a cop. My mother was a cop. I have five cousins who were cops. They all died at the hands of costumed criminals. So I started the Crimefighters to take back the city. I recruited Nina —

NINA. The Arch Public Enemy killed my brother.

SALLY. And Jazmin.

JAZMIN. I just like to beat up men.

SALLY. And now I'm asking you to join us and be a Crimefighter.

LISA. Oh!

JAZMIN. We would teach you everything you need to know.

NINA. I lead a seminar.

JAZMIN. You would have all the tools you need.

NINA. And a costume.

SALLY. Join us. With you on our side, we'll bring Doctor X to his knees.

LISA. I don't know.

SALLY. What don't you know? It's your calling.

LISA. Yeah, it's just. I've just sort of started seeing someone.

SALLY. Oh.

NINA, JAZMIN. Oh.

LISA. And I don't know if it would be fair to him to put him in danger. To put myself in danger.

SALLY. It's a difficult decision. I mean on one hand, you could help to protect the world from criminals and those who think life is cheap.

JAZMIN. Or she could follow her heart. *(The Crimefighters sigh in unison as they think about what it is to follow one's heart.)*

LISA. I do have a lot of time on my hands.

18

SALLY. Right.

LISA. I am looking to do something useful with my days.

JAZMIN. Sure.

LISA. I do want the world to be safe for lovers.

SALLY. Of course you do. Spectacular women such as ourselves, women in danger usually live solitary lives. It's just the way it goes. There are exceptions of course. Nina used to date a man of the law.

NINA. It was a quiet romance. Until the Jolly Puzzler drowned him in acid.

JAZMIN. Sally used to date the commissioner.

SALLY. That was a long time ago.

NINA. Not that long.

JAZMIN. I have a lot of one-night stands.

SALLY. All of this is to say, you have to figure it out for yourself. The world is dangerous. Love is scarce. Crime is prevalent. *(A silence. Lisa considers.)*

LISA. I can't. No, I can't. I'm sorry.

SALLY. Well we're sorry to hear that.

JAZMIN. Very sorry.

NINA. Here's our card if you change your mind. *(Lisa takes the card. They all look at one another.)*

SALLY. Well, I guess we should go then.

JAZMIN. Hope we see you again.

NINA. Yeah, me too.

LISA. Thank you. *(Lisa exits to the restaurant. She goes to the table. She sees Peter's coat is gone. She realizes he is not returning. She doesn't understand, but it hurts.)*

5

In the hospital, the nurses stand around talking. Peter is visible in a space behind them, working on an artificial heart with a screwdriver.

PETER. Beat, dammit!

SALLY. Is he in there again?

NURSE. Yeah. Never eats or sleeps, just plays with that darn heart.

NINA. Does it work?

JAZMIN. Not yet.

NURSE. If he's fiddling around with that, he doesn't have to deal with the world outside or with real problems or with other people.

SALLY. He's solving a real problem.

NURSE. He's running away.

SALLY. You're not being fair.

NURSE. I don't want to be fair to him. He's never been fair to me.

NINA. Can you say that? Can you really say that?

NURSE. If he'd been fair to me, He would have let me kiss him under the mistletoe at the Christmas party. He would have smiled back more, he would have frowned less. He would have taken the time to notice my body instead of looking away. He's never been fair to me, so he doesn't know what could have happened.

NINA. I guess he's never been fair to me either, now that you mention it.

SALLY. He has a higher calling.

NURSE. He has an escape hatch. I wish I had one. I would have liked to have found it in his lips. *(The nurses sigh in unison.)*

JAZMIN. His lips.

SALLY. His lips.

NINA. His lips.

PETER. Dammit! Why won't you beat? Beat! Beat! *(Peter fiddles with it some more.)*

NURSE. I've seen him in there, you know.

NINA. You have?

SALLY. When?

NURSE. I seen him with the heart. Hitting it with the hammer. Shimmying his screwdriver between the chambers.

PETER. Beat, dammit. Beat.

SALLY. He wants the heart to beat for him, but a heart will only beat for who a heart beats for.

NINA. Isn't that the truth? *(Nurse agrees but says nothing.)*

6

Nurse moves into another scene where Doctor X is in the bed. Nurse gets under the sheets with him. This is a flashback. They are post-coital.

DOCTOR X. Well that was —
NURSE. Yeah.
DOCTOR X. You're a firecracker.
NURSE. Thank you.
DOCTOR X. A firecracker with a face like a plate.
NURSE. What?
DOCTOR X. That was such a surprise.
NURSE. For me too.
DOCTOR X. But now that it's happened —
NURSE. I should go.
DOCTOR X. Don't go. You're intoxicating.
NURSE. Thank you.
DOCTOR X. You're refreshing.
NURSE. Thank you.
DOCTOR X. You're delightful.
NURSE. Okay. *(Doctor X holds Nurse. She lets him.)*
DOCTOR X. How did I get so lucky to have you in my arms?
NURSE. I'm not sure. I mean I'm always fragile after a patient dies. That's certain. So something like this was bound to happen. And your hands. I've been watching of course your hands every time in surgery and they are so sure. So certain. You trust something so confident. Even when they wander and you're not sure what they're doing, you go with it, because of the skill.
DOCTOR X. Yes, these hands are my curse and my blessing.
NURSE. They're very beautiful.
DOCTOR X. No, they aren't.
NURSE. What happens with us tomorrow?
DOCTOR X. What do you mean?
NURSE. When we first see each other, what will happen? Will you turn away?

DOCTOR X. No.

NURSE. Will I hide my face?

DOCTOR X. Why would you?

NURSE. Do you think this will happen again?

DOCTOR X. Of course.

NURSE. You may be right. I am someone who makes the same mistakes over and over. It's my nature. If this is a mistake, I might make it twenty times before I learn my lesson.

DOCTOR X. I wish all mistakes were like this.

NURSE. All my mistakes are like this.

DOCTOR X. *(An outburst, kind of scary.)* Don't say that! This is not a mistake! It's not! Tell me it's not a mistake!

NURSE. It's not a mistake.

DOCTOR X. Of course it's not. This is love.

NURSE. It is?

DOCTOR X. Yes! It is! Tell me it's love!

NURSE. It's love!

DOCTOR X. I'm going to hold you forever. Forever.

NURSE. You're hurting me.

DOCTOR X. Shhh. Shhh.

NURSE. Ow.

DOCTOR X. You'll learn to like it. I save people's lives with these hands. These arms. You'll learn to enjoy whatever they do.

NURSE. Oh. Ow. Oh.

DOCTOR X. I learned when I was young, if you want to keep something, hold it tight and never let it go because if you don't keep your things close, someone will come and take them away. I won't let that happen to you now that I've found you.

NURSE. You won't?

DOCTOR X. No, I won't. I won't let you go. Never let you go. Never. Never. *(Nurse gets up and walks away. The flashback ends. We are in the present and Doctor X is in his bed. He awakes alone.)* Where did you go? How could you go? I was holding so tightly. You will pay! You will all pay! No one will have love unless I have love!!! You hear me?!! You hear me, world?! *(Doctor X gets his doctor's bag. He loads a syringe, tests it and exits into the night.)*

7

Lisa walks down the street in a fog. Sound of men whistling and catcalls. She keeps walking. A car screeching and a huge crash as the car hits something. Car alarms.

MAN. *(Offstage.)* Hey lady, do us all a favor and go inside.
LISA. Sorry. *(Lisa continues to walk. As she speaks, there may be more catcalls, sounds of men walking into posts and mailboxes.)* What is this feeling, so unpleasant, like my insides rotting or my outside melting? There is a bad taste in my mouth that won't go away. I feel itchy and oversized and everything is crawling. Is this what rejection is? Isn't there usually a heaviness to it? An unbearable weight? *(Beat.)* Oh, there it is. A big boat of depression sailing over my chest. It hurts. It hurts so much. It's not — is it me? No one has ever rejected me before. He must be a lunatic. He must be some sort of nutcase. Someone not all there, because why else — ? Ohhh. Or he can see everything wrong with me, all the things I'm afraid are there but can forget about. He knows I'm no good. I could have fought Doctor X harder. I could have climbed the fire escape faster maybe. Or I could have tried harder to love them back. If I had made myself maybe or — *(Peter at the table, working on the heart. The nurses nearby.)*
PETER. Beat, dammit, beat.
NURSE. I have a plan.
SALLY. You do?
NINA. You do?
JAZMIN. You do?
NURSE. He came home early from the date. This is good news.
SALLY, NINA, JAZMIN. Right.
NURSE. It means it went badly. But, I know not to go in there while he's working. I know not to hang around after either.
SALLY. Unless he gets it to work.
JAZMIN. If he got it to work, he would be so happy probably he might want to celebrate and then you could celebrate with him. If you know what I mean.
NURSE. You're bad.

JAZMIN. I know.

NURSE. She's bad.

NINA. I know.

NURSE. I can't wait around. My shift will be over. My feet are sore. My back is sore. I'm tired and hungry. It might beat tonight sure, but I get off in ten minutes and I'm not sticking around for two hours, three hours, four hours.

JAZMIN. No, I suppose not. But what could happen is that he will get it to work and want to celebrate and then he will celebrate with whoever happens to be nearby.

NURSE. I didn't think about that.

PETER. I don't have to think when I'm working. I don't have to feel. Memories and guilt and sadness all slide away because they don't fit in my head when I'm working. Beat! Beat! I don't have to remember climbing in the laundry pile and sobbing after they leave. I don't have to remember the way Lisa smells or the taste of her lipstick on my lips after her kiss. Or her laugh, always startling, but runs right through you. I don't have to think about what a coward I am, or how magnetic she is. Or the damage she may have already done to my heart — stopping it one time, two times, three times. I don't have a heart that can stop on a dime I don't have a — Beat! Beat! I should try a different power source.

NURSE. Your shift is just starting.

SALLY. It is.

NURSE. You could call me if it happens. You have my pager. Any time. If it happens, I'll hop on my Vespa and be here in two minutes.

SALLY. Okay.

NURSE. Promise me?

SALLY. I promise. But it won't happen tonight.

NINA. No.

JAZMIN. No, it won't.

NURSE. And tomorrow, tomorrow I will go up to him and I will say, "Peter we are going out to dinner and I won't take no for an answer."

NINA. You'll say that?

NURSE. If she can do it, I can do it.

JAZMIN. That's your plan?

NURSE. And I'll tell you another thing. He won't be back here an hour later working on that heart.

SALLY. You said it.

PETER. Beat! Beat!

NURSE. I will give him a night to remember. *(Lisa continues to walk. The catcalls continue.)*
LISA. What do people do after they get rejected? Do they curl into a ball and die? Do they tear out their hair? Drink themselves into oblivion? I want to do all of these things at once. There must be something outstanding about him if he's too good for me. Now I will never want anyone besides him. All other men are fools and idiots who could never measure up. No, there is nothing to do now except commit to a life of celibacy. A life with meaning. *(She takes out her cell phone and dials the number on the card the Crimefighters gave her.)* Hello, Crimefighters? *(A huge crash.)*

8

Sally, Jazmin and Nina enter doing backflips, cartwheels, or swinging swords, nun-chucks. They take turns sparring with Lisa who is given various weapons to defend herself. She backs away from each of them in turn, stumbles, gets beaten down.

SALLY. Keep your defenses up!
JAZMIN. Don't let your guard down.
NINA. You're leaving yourself open!
SALLY. You're letting us get too close.
NINA. Keep your guard up.
JAZMIN. Don't let your defenses down.
SALLY. I shouldn't be able to touch you.
JAZMIN. I shouldn't be anywhere near you.
SALLY. You got to keep everyone away.
NINA. Keep your hands up.
SALLY. Expect the unexpected.
NINA. If you're not alert —
JAZMIN. If you're not paying attention —
NINA. You will get hurt.
JAZMIN. They will hurt you.
SALLY. They will all hurt you.
NINA. Unless you prevent it.

25

SALLY. By keeping them away. By defending yourself from them.

JAZMIN. No one should be able to get to you. *(The sparring continues over the following. This time, Lisa attacks and gets the upper hand. She makes them each fall in turn.)*

LISA. What about always being on the offensive? I never have to defend if I'm always attacking. I'm the kind of girl who has never had to protect herself because I'm the first to make the move. I will preempt your preemptive strike. I will get the drop on you. You will see me coming and you will scramble for a defense, except that I'm already past your defenses. The moment you take to collect yourself is a moment too many. I've learned what my looks can do and I've taken every opportunity presented. And the opportunities keep presenting themselves. I may not know how to defend, but it's only because I've never had to until now.

JAZMIN. Wow.

NINA. Ohh.

SALLY. Where did you learn that?

LISA. What, you mean the fighting? I picked it up somewhere or other.

SALLY. However you learned it, you're ready. *(Sally straps a gadget to Lisa's wrist.)* This has a homing device on it.

JAZMIN. Never take it off.

SALLY. If you're ever in danger, press this button and we'll all come find you.

NINA. You'll never have to face danger alone again.

LISA. Thank you.

SALLY. Now you're ready to begin. *(They all take a deep breath.)* Ready?

NINA. Ready.

JAZMIN. Ready.

LISA. Ready.

SALLY. Nina, you take Lisa and I'll take Jazmin and we'll hit the streets. Our patrols are the only thing keeping this city off the brink of chaos. Glad we've got one more Crimefighter out there keeping the streets safe. Oh and here, you'll need this. *(Sally tosses Lisa a mask. She catches it, puts it on.)*

9

Nina and Lisa scour the streets in full Crimefighter getup. Normal city noises.

LISA. There aren't any accidents.

NINA. What?

LISA. No one is shouting at me.

NINA. Why would they shout at you?

LISA. Right. I mean I guess it's this mask. They think I'm one of you. So they look at me but they can look away. They don't run red lights or walk into passerbys. Because I'm a known quantity now. A Crimefighter.

NINA. Yes.

LISA. It feels great. I feel free. No one told me being anonymous was so much fun.

NINA. It's one of the secrets of being a crimefighting hero.

LISA. What are the other secrets?

NINA. Oh, you'll learn soon enough. Lots of free drinks. Cutting in line at the movies.

LISA. That already happens to me.

NINA. Oh.

LISA. But now it will be because of what I do instead of what I look like.

NINA. Oh.

LISA. No more men for me.

NINA. No?

LISA. How do you do it?

NINA. Oh, you get used to it.

LISA. I mean, there have been men?

NINA. Oh, sure. Sure. Well, no. Not in a long time. And honestly, I don't miss it. Or rather, the job has taken over for providing me with that excitement. And there's nothing that beats crimefighting. I don't care what kind of sex you've had.

LISA. I've had lots of kinds.

NINA. We all have. Well, I haven't, but you can't go by me. I mean actually, the thing about me is, and please don't say anything to the others —

LISA. I won't.

NINA. The thing is, ever since my run in with Doctor X, well, he's all I can think about. I can't stop thinking about the Doctor. Day and night. When I'm brushing my teeth. Even when — you know.

LISA. Oh.

NINA. Doctor X is just so exciting. And wrong. So exciting and wrong. I think the other girls have an inkling. Because I — I let him get away. I paused. If you know me, you know I'm not someone who ever pauses. I run into any situation, burning building, shark-infested pool, without a thought. But I saw Doctor X and I paused, to the point of stopping even. And it was not revulsion I was feeling. Well, it was, but it was mixed with something else, something potent. I'm not sure what. They should bottle it if they could ever find a way to collect it. They'd make millions.

LISA. Who?

NINA. Exactly. *(Doctor X enters here as Nina's memory and they look at each other.)* He just stood there, looking at me, with his doctor's bag and syringe. He showed no remorse. Remorseless. Soulless maybe. And it took my breath away. I'm terrified of what might happen the next time I run into him. You have to be ready at all times to kill if necessary. But when I think — I'm not sure I could do it in this case. I dread our next meeting and at the same time I look forward to it more than anything in my entire life. You know what I mean?

LISA. Yes.

10

Lisa and Nina exit. Doctor X becomes real. Doctor X approaches a sleeping couple who have arrived surreptitiously. He prepares his needles.

DOCTOR X. I don't have to think when I'm working. I don't have to feel. I don't get angry about the things I can't remember because all I need to know is the work in front of me. Everyone will pay! And the things I can remember don't haunt me. Her face like a plate. Her disappearance. Or her laugh, always startling, but runs right through you. Or who I am. Who am I? I don't have to think about that now. I have lovers to kill. I can concentrate on the damage I will inflict. You will all pay! There is something satisfying about an accomplished task. How can you be ever truly depressed if you accomplish all you set out to do? Some days it's just enough to get out of bed. Or to kill a couple of people. No more. Yes the refrigerator is empty but as long as something was accomplished, well then, it's back to bed. A sleep and maybe in the morning, a remembering. A thought about my mother. A vision of a room. And her, always her, with a face you want to eat off. *(He injects them both.)* Well that's done.

11

Doctor X exits. The Crimefighters and Lisa arrive at the slain couple. It is a crime scene now. They all put on rubber gloves as they enter. The dummies of the previous scene are replaced by Carson and Ed.

SALLY. Welcome to your first crime scene.
LISA. It's — not like I thought.
SALLY. It never is.
JAZMIN. Doctor X entered through the window as is his custom. He stood here.
NINA. I'm standing where Doctor X stood. I'm breathing the same air. It feels — I don't know. I feel alive.
JAZMIN. The Doctor is efficient. I'll say that. Comes in. Kills 'em. Goes out.
NINA. It makes me shiver.
SALLY. Any clues?
JAZMIN. Nothing.
LISA. *(Standing over the dead couple.)* Look at his eyelashes. He reminds me of —

JAZMIN. Who?

LISA. No one. Never mind. I shouldn't think of it anyway.

NINA. You can't help what you think.

LISA. Can't I?

SALLY. Get some carpet samples.

NINA. I'll take samples of where I'm standing.

JAZMIN. I have a sink full of dishes at home. Why do I always think of that at a crime scene?

SALLY. I always think of the commissioner.

NINA. I think of nothing but Doctor X.

LISA. They were very much in love. *(The Crimefighters gather around the dead bodies.)*

SALLY. They were?

JAZMIN. Were they?

LISA. The way they're holding each other.

NINA. I don't see it.

LISA. Look how close they were. Breathing on each other until they stopped. Oh, yeah, there's no doubt. They were very much in love. *(A flashback: The couple, Ed and Carson, come alive. Carson in bed. Ed moving around. It is staged in such a way that we don't see Carson's face.)*

CARSON. Come to bed.

ED. I'm coming.

CARSON. Did you lock the window?

ED. Yesss. I always lock the window.

CARSON. Did you lock the window tonight?

ED. I said I locked the window.

CARSON. Okay. Okay. Don't get bent out of shape.

ED. I'm not.

CARSON. Are you sure I'm the one you want to spend the rest of your life with?

ED. I'm sure.

CARSON. Are you sure you're sure?

ED. Yes.

CARSON. I'm sure, too.

ED. Let's go to sleep.

CARSON. Okay. Hold me. *(They hold one another.)* Our life is good.

ED. I think so.

CARSON. Me too.

ED. You were really good at Trivial Pursuit tonight. *(But Carson is asleep. Ed closes his eyes. Light shift. They are dead again. The Crime-fighters and Lisa sigh.)*

LISA. It makes you think.

SALLY, JAZMIN. Yeah.

LISA. Oh, well.

NINA. What's wrong with me?

SALLY. Why did I ever break it off with the commissioner?

LISA. I think I'm going to cry.

NINA. I'm alone.

JAZMIN. I'm going to be late to my date. But I ran out of fabric softener. Should I go get the fabric softener and be a little later and then carry it around on the date? Or should I just go without it and have clothes that aren't as soft?

LISA. I can't stand this.

SALLY. I think I'm going to call the commissioner and say we should give it another shot.

LISA. I got to go.

JAZMIN. Are you going?

LISA. I can't wait another second. I'm sorry. *(The Crimefighters watch her go.)*

12

The hospital. The Crimefighters, now nurses hang around Peter. Nurse stands behind him, building up the courage. The others urge her on.

JAZMIN. Go on.

NINA. Go on.

SALLY. You can do it.

NURSE. Yes I can. No, I can't. Yes. Okay. Yes. Peter?

PETER. *(Looking at a file.)* Mmm?

NURSE. Peter, can I talk to you?

PETER. What is it?

NURSE. Well, it's —

PETER. Yes?

31

NURSE. Um … I wanted to ask — *(Enter Lisa. She steps between Nurse and Peter.)*

LISA. No one leaves me like that.

PETER. I'm sorry.

LISA. I walked all the way here, rehearsing what I was going to say to you. But now I don't remember any of it. I know you're afraid. Well, you may find this hard to believe, but I'm afraid, too. Standing here in front of you like this is the scariest thing I've ever done. But here I am. Because I don't want to live an incomplete life, and a life without you is incomplete. I refuse to let my fear and your fear keep us from being together.

PETER. Well —

LISA. I think if there is the slightest chance this thing can work between the two of us, we need to go at it with everything we got. Because tomorrow we could be dead and then it's too late. I don't know about you but I'd rather die in your arms than alone. It's just what I want. And I think it's what you want, too, if you could get past the conflicted emotions you have and the worry you feel for your heart. What do you think? No, wait. *(Lisa kisses him.)* Now what do you think?

PETER. Okay, let's do it.

LISA. All right.

PETER. I'm shaking.

LISA. Me too. *(Exit Peter and Lisa.)*

JAZMIN. Well, that didn't go well. *(Nurse begins to cry.)*

SALLY. There, there. It's not your fault. You just can't compete with that.

NURSE. I know! *(Nurse cries harder.)*

13

Lisa and Peter at Lisa's place.

LISA. You're worried. I can see that you're worried. I'm going to try not to hurt you.

PETER. I appreciate it. *(Lisa puts his stethoscope around her neck.*

Then she kisses him. Lisa listens to his heart after the kiss.)
LISA. I think you're okay. We can try it again. *(They kiss some more.)* You know what? I think this isn't fair. I'm casting a spell with my kiss. How can you think straight when I'm here?
PETER. Oh.
LISA. Maybe it's not true until I go away again.
PETER. Don't go.
LISA. I don't want to be making decisions for you. I want to make sure it's something we both want. And are both willing to fight for.
PETER. Oh.
LISA. You know what I mean?
PETER. Yeah.
LISA. I'm going to go to the bathroom. I'll be gone long enough for you to think but not much longer than that. I don't want you to go, but if you have to go, please go now. It will hurt us both less later.
PETER. Okay.
LISA. I just remembered what happened the last time I went to the bathroom.
PETER. Oh. Yeah.
LISA. All the same, I'll go now and you can work and rework your fears. Remember the feeling of me in your arms. Remember to live for right now. Oh, I don't know. I've said enough. *(Lisa exits. Peter sits there, a little dumbfounded. In the hospital, Nina, Sally and Jazmin console Nurse.)*
NURSE. It hurts.
SALLY. There there.
NINA. You're okay.
JAZMIN. You're gonna be okay. *(Sally listens to Nurse's heart.)*
NURSE. How does it sound?
SALLY. You're gonna be fine.
NURSE. Can I get a CAT scan?
SALLY. No.
NINA. You want me to take over your shift?
NURSE. Would you?
NINA. If you want.
NURSE. No, that's okay. I guess I'll just have a doughnut. *(Back at Lisa's place, Peter has not left. Lisa returns from the bathroom wearing much less than when she exited.)*
LISA. You're still here.

PETER. Yes.

LISA. So you'll stay?

PETER. Right now, I'll stay. There's a bolting part of me that wants to bolt, and maybe that will always be a problem. But right now, I'm going to stay and I'm going to try to keep staying.

LISA. I guess I can't ask anything more. *(Lisa kisses him.)*

PETER. Listen to my heart. *(Lisa listens to his heart. They kiss some more. They are really going at it. Lisa stops, listens to his heart. She nods. They continue going at it. They begin to remove their clothing. After every piece of removed clothing, Lisa listens to his heart to make sure they can continue. They get under the covers. In the hospital the nurses all eat doughnuts.)*

14

At the Crimefighter base of operations.

VOICE OF COMMISSIONER. Crimefighters!

SALLY, JAZMIN, NINA. Commissioner!

VOICE OF COMMISSIONER. Where's the new one?

NINA. Oh, she's —

SALLY. Otherwise occupied at the moment.

NINA. She's been kind of busy the last couple of weeks.

JAZMIN. She'll be back.

NINA. You're cynical.

SALLY. You wanted to speak to us, Commissioner?

VOICE OF COMMISSIONER. Yes, yes. We need to step up our search for Doctor X.

JAZMIN. What else do you want us to do?

NINA. We're doing everything we can.

VOICE OF COMMISSIONER. I'm putting more of the force on the case. I'm having rookies watch fire escapes.

SALLY. There are too many fire escapes.

JAZMIN. *(Suggestively.)* And not enough rookies.

VOICE OF COMMISSIONER. I know. But Doctor X has killed a couple of lovers every day this week. It can't go on!

SALLY. If we only knew where Doctor X's lair was. *(The Crimefighters all sigh.)*
VOICE OF COMMISSIONER. Thank you, Crimefighters. I know you're doing everything you can.
JAZMIN, NINA. We are.
VOICE OF COMMISSIONER. Unfortunately, that's just not enough.
SALLY. We'll try harder.
VOICE OF COMMISSIONER. Good.
SALLY. Good.
VOICE OF COMMISSIONER. So, um, Sally.
SALLY. Commissioner.
VOICE OF COMMISSIONER. About your email.
SALLY. Yes? *(Nina and Jazmin turn away awkwardly to give a bit of privacy.)*
VOICE OF COMMISSIONER. I don't know quite what to say.
SALLY. Oh.
VOICE OF COMMISSIONER. Except, you know, I appreciate you, um, contacting me and everything.
SALLY. Oh.
VOICE OF COMMISSIONER. And that I feel the same way.
SALLY. Oh!
VOICE OF COMMISSIONER. I mean, we'll have to resolve some of our issues.
SALLY. Of course.
VOICE OF COMMISSIONER. But I think it's worth the work.
SALLY. I agree.
VOICE OF COMMISSIONER. Are you free Friday night?
SALLY. Yes! Oh, no. Friday's a little rough.
VOICE OF COMMISSIONER. Saturday?
SALLY. This Saturday? No. Prime Doctor X time.
VOICE OF COMMISSIONER. Oh, right. Sunday?
SALLY. I wish I could.
VOICE OF COMMISSIONER. Next week at all?
SALLY. Thursday?
VOICE OF COMMISSIONER. I can't do Thursday. The mayor has something. Say, you wouldn't want to — no, no. It's not any fun. You couldn't do Tuesday?
SALLY. My sister's baby shower.
VOICE OF COMMISSIONER. Oh. Lunch Wednesday?

SALLY. I have something, but no. You know what? I'm going to cancel. Yes, lunch Wednesday.

VOICE OF COMMISSIONER. Oh, I can't Wednesday. What am I thinking? I'm such an idiot. How about Friday?

SALLY. Not this week, but next?

VOICE OF COMMISSIONER. Right.

SALLY. I can't. But yes. I don't care. Next Friday. Any time.

VOICE OF COMMISSIONER. Excellent. Friday.

SALLY. Next Friday.

VOICE OF COMMISSIONER. Right. Good! I look forward to it.

SALLY. Me too!

VOICE OF COMMISSIONER. Okay. Bye, then.

SALLY. Bye! *(Jazmin and Nina gather around Sally to celebrate what just happened.)*

15

In Peter's apartment. Lisa and Peter are in bed together.

LISA. Tell me about my heart.

PETER. Make a fist. *(She does. He holds it in his hand. He kisses it.)*

LISA. Ooh.

PETER. Your heart is about the size of your fist. Your cute little fist.

LISA. This fist?

PETER. That fist. Or the other fist. Either of your cute little fists.

LISA. What else?

PETER. The heart is not nailed down. It's an organ that can move this way or that. No one knows which direction it will go. The heart is unpredictable.

LISA. That's my heart. Very unpredictable. That's why I've had so many lovers. Sometimes the heart goes here. Sometimes there. And I come tumbling after … I've upset you. *(During this, Peter has stood to go.)*

PETER. *(Upset.)* No. I just … have work to do.

LISA. Don't work now.

PETER. I have to. The world needs a dependable artificial heart.

LISA. Sure, but you don't have to be the first test subject. What if you never wake up?

PETER. Well, first let me get the heart to work and then we'll talk surgery. Right now I have to get back to work. If I can save one life it'll be worth all the late nights and sacrifice.

LISA. Do you have to go right now?

PETER. Well …

LISA. *(Flirty.)* Couldn't you stay a bit longer?

PETER. I guess I could stay a bit longer. *(Peter climbs back in bed with her. They get comfortable. They begin to kiss maybe. Just then, the Crimefighter alert strapped to Lisa's wrist starts to glow bright red and beep loudly.)* What's that?

LISA. Oh, nothing. *(Lisa jumps up to get dressed.)*

PETER. What are you doing?

LISA. I have to go.

PETER. Where?

LISA. I can't tell you. I just have to go! *(And she goes.)*

16

Lisa patrols the street with Nina. Peter goes to his work area and works on the heart.

NINA. They saw Doctor X near here they said. Can you feel how the air is charged? It's like liquid electricity all over my face … my body. *(To unseen guy off.)* What are you looking at buddy? Keep walking. *(She goes back to feeling the air on her skin.)*

LISA. So I can't ever tell anyone I'm a Crimefighter?

NINA. Huh? I'm sorry, what?

LISA. I can't ever tell anyone I'm a Crimefighter?

NINA. No, you can't. It would compromise us all.

LISA. It's just —

NINA. You want to tell him.

LISA. Yeah.

NINA. The Commissioner, of course, already knows, but Sally swears the Commissioner only knows her as a Crimefighter. She says she wears the mask to the movie theater even.

LISA. The Commissioner doesn't know her true identity?

NINA. Well, that can't be true. I mean there's no way, right? Between you and me, I think she just thinks the mask gives her a certain mystery. Shhh! Be still. No, never mind. It's just a rat.

LISA. I can't live like this.

NINA. You know you think you can't but really you can. When it comes down to it, people always think they can't go on, but they do, you know?

LISA. Yeah.

NINA. Ohhh! Can you feel the air? Doctor X was here all right. It's intense.

LISA. I can see that. What are you going to do?

NINA. About the Doctor? I don't know. What will you do about your Doctor?

LISA. I don't know. I feel him pulling away sometimes.

NINA. Oh.

LISA. And I'm just afraid he might go away and not come back. He's protecting himself, I know.

NINA. Sure.

LISA. But he has to let me get close. Otherwise, well, what's the point?

NINA. Right.

LISA. I don't know. What should I do?

NINA. Enjoy every second he's there. And if he goes, he will go. But you will have enjoyed the time he was there.

LISA. Yeah.

NINA. He'll come around.

LISA. You think?

NINA. Oh, I have no idea.

LISA. Oh.

NINA. At the very least, be happy you're obsessed with someone who wants to spend time with you. My obsession would probably try to kill me. And you know, I might even let him. Doctor X, what are you doing right now? Where are you? *(Doctor X in a spot, loads a hypodermic. The Doctor is sad. The spot goes out.)*

17

Nurse is eating doughnuts. Sally, Nina and Jazmin watch.

NINA. You've been eating lots of doughnuts.
NURSE. Not really.
NINA. Yes, really.
NURSE. I know but I have good reasons.
JAZMIN. What's a good reason to eat so many doughnuts?
NURSE. You know why I do it. It's him.
SALLY. You're eating too many. It's not good for you. That many doughnuts takes a toll on your heart. I know you think you can hurt your heart, get your arteries clogged, have a heart attack so he'll operate on you, but that's not the way. That way will lead you to nowhere but pain.
NURSE. But —
JAZMIN. You need to let up on the doughnuts. We've all noticed. It's become too much.
NINA. We're concerned.
NURSE. You're concerned?
JAZMIN. This is an intervention.
NURSE. It is?
NINA. Miriam wanted to come but she's in surgery.
NURSE. With a doctor.
SALLY. Yes.
NURSE. Thank you for your intervention. I'm touched. I'm warmed. My heart ... But I don't know how to fill myself if I stop eating doughnuts. I'm afraid I will cease to exist if I stop eating even for a minute.
SALLY. We're here to help you.
NINA. Tell us what you want us to do.
JAZMIN. We can go out for a healthy lunch. Together. Would you like that?
NURSE. Okay. *(Enter Peter, ecstatic.)*
PETER. It works! The heart works! *(Peter hugs everyone but Nurse, jumps up and down in celebration.)* The heartbeat is so strong, much

stronger than I thought it would be.

NURSE. That's great!

PETER. I have to go tell Lisa! *(Peter exits running. Nurse breaks down and sobs.)*

NURSE. AHHHHHHH!

SALLY. Okay. It's okay. We can have another intervention tomorrow. *(Nina offers her a doughnut.)*

18

Peter and Lisa in Peter's bedroom.

PETER. You're unhappy.

LISA. No, that's great! I'm really happy for you. You did it. It's something to be proud of.

PETER. But …

LISA. But nothing. Tonight we will have wild angry sex. Or I will at least. It will be fantastic. You will thank God you were born and then tomorrow you will go under anesthesia and never come back.

PETER. Not this again. I need a new heart. You know that. It's been broken so many times —

LISA. Not anymore.

PETER. Can you promise that?

LISA. I can promise you to love you the best I can for as long as I can. Will that work?

PETER. Where did you go yesterday?

LISA. Oh. I can't tell you.

PETER. You say I'm pulling away.

LISA. There are certain things I can't tell you about myself.

PETER. Ever?

LISA. Ever. For your protection. The knowledge would endanger you.

PETER. You want me to put everything into this relationship but you refuse to do the same.

LISA. You just have to trust me.

PETER. Can you trust me on the heart? That I will survive a little bit of heart surgery?
LISA. How do you know that?
PETER. I just know.
LISA. I'll trust you. Just don't do it tomorrow. Wait a day, will you?
PETER. A day?
LISA. Or two.
PETER. If it's that important to you.
LISA. Yes.
PETER. I'll wait. But eventually —
LISA. Let's not talk about eventually. I promised you angry sex.
(They kiss. It is passionate.)

19

Peter's apartment. Later. They sleep. Doctor X enters, looks at them, opens the doctor's bag, takes out a syringe.

DOCTOR X. Shh. You won't feel a thing. You would thank me if you could. Both of you. "Thank you," you would say, "for killing me now while I'm happy." "Later," you will tell me, "Later my lover will disappoint me. Will leave me or trap me or make me wish I were dead, so thank you for killing me now and making permanent this moment of perfection." Yes, that's what you would say. I know. I've been there. There was a girl once with a face like a plate. She was beautiful. She was everything and then one day I remember … No, I don't remember. I remember — no, I don't. She was, I think — no. So it is better you go like this than like that. This is the best way. I took an oath. I think I took an oath: to help people. So there is no need to thank me, though I know you would if you could. It is all part of the good work I do. So sleep soundly. Enjoy each other's arms. You won't feel a thing. *(Doctor X is about to inject Peter when Lisa wakes and sees him.)*
LISA. You!
DOCTOR X. You! *(There is a struggle. Doctor X tries to inject Peter and Lisa prevents him. During the fight, Lisa manages to press her*

wrist contraption which then glows and beeps. If possible, we may see the other three Crimefighters in the middle of something when their wrists begin to pulse. One is washing dishes. One is jogging. One is eating a sandwich. Or something. They drop what they are doing and come to join the fight already in progress. Sally gets there first and joins Lisa just when it looked like she was done for.) A Crimefighter!

SALLY. That's right!

DOCTOR X. Take this, Crimefighter! *(Doctor X attacks. It is pretty scary.)*

SALLY. Where did you learn that?

DOCTOR X. I don't remember. *(They fight. Nina arrives next. She sees Doctor X.)*

NINA. It's him! *(Nina freezes. She is needed in the fight but she is unable to move. Jazmin arrives and sees Nina.)*

JAZMIN. Snap out of it! Hey! *(Nina does snap out of it and they both join the fight. What follows is a gargantuan fight. Every jujitsu move. Fun weapons. It can be heart-pounding and exciting or stylized and lyrical but it must be something fun to watch and should go on for a while. During the fight, Peter wakes up. He tries to help.)*

PETER. What's going on?

SALLY. *(To Peter.)* Stay back!

PETER. Should I —

SALLY. No! Leave it to the professionals!

PETER. But —

SALLY. *(Pushing him down.)* Sit! *(Peter sits and watches the fight. One by one the Crimefighters fight Doctor X and fall. But they get back up and come back at him. Then, one of them makes Doctor X fall.)*

DOCTOR X. Ahhh! *(They surround him.)*

SALLY. We've been waiting a long time for this.

JAZMIN. We have.

SALLY. You're coming downtown with us.

DOCTOR X. No, I don't think so. I think this time, you are mistaken. *(Doctor X injects himself and then slumps over seemingly dead. Peter rushes over to check Doctor X's vitals.)*

PETER. Stand back. Stand back. I need space. *(Peter checks.)*

LISA. Well?

PETER. The heart stopped. *(To Lisa.)* Go in the study and get my heart.

LISA. It's here?

PETER. I couldn't be away from it. *(Lisa rushes off.)*

NINA. Is there anything we can do?

PETER. You, go to the kitchen and boil some water. Find the sharpest knives and sterilize them. The salad tongs too. Whatever's in there. Best to just boil all the kitchen utensils. You, call the hospital and tell them I have an emergency here and I need a chopper. You, get a bunch of towels. Wash your hands. And then rush back here. I'm going to need all the help I can get. *(They rush off to their tasks. Lisa returns with the artificial heart in her hands.)*

LISA. Here it is.

PETER. Thank you.

LISA. It's beautiful.

PETER. Thank you.

LISA. It's — I

PETER. Not now. Right now, I have to save a life. Later we can talk. *(The lights change. A surgery scene. This should have the same energy and intensity as the fight scene did. The Crimefighters all have their hands or utensils in Doctor X and Peter is telling them what to do. This can be partially or completely behind a scrim. It begins without sound. Peter is feverishly working and so are the others but we don't hear him. There is music perhaps or the beating of the heart. Then it's like the sound is suddenly turned on. Peter is putting the heart in.)* Good. Good. I need you to squeeze those salad tongs harder. The ice tongs too. Good. More towels. I need a sharper knife. Excellent. Okay. Okay. Okay. Good. There. Good. Okay. It's in! It's in. It's beating. It's so strong. Good work, ladies. You were all amazing. You might think about careers in the nursing field. I mean, if you weren't so busy.

JAZMIN. Well, actually — *(Sally kicks her.)*

PETER. What?

JAZMIN. Nothing. *(Sound of the chopper arriving overhead.)*

SALLY. Now, what?

PETER. Now we close him up. You can let go. I can take it from here.

NINA. And then?

PETER. To the hospital. You'll want to guard him, I imagine.

SALLY. Yes. Nina, Jazmin. You rest. I'll take the first shift.

LISA. What about me?

SALLY. Well, I assumed. I assumed, you would come along. There are conversations you want to have, perhaps. You have things to say. *(Lisa and Peter look at each other.)*

20

The hospital. Sally stands guard outside Doctor X's room. Nurse enters with medication on a tray.

SALLY. What do you got there?

NURSE. It's for sleeping.

SALLY. Okay, go ahead.

NURSE. Thanks. *(Nurse enters the room. Doctor X is handcuffed to the bed. They look at each other for a long time. Neither of them moves. Then, finally, Nurse approaches.)* I have medication for you. It'll allow you to sleep.

DOCTOR X. It's you.

NURSE. Yes.

DOCTOR X. It's really you.

NURSE. Yes.

DOCTOR X. I can't believe it.

NURSE. I didn't know if you'd know me.

DOCTOR X. I couldn't ever forget you.

NURSE. I thought you might.

DOCTOR X. I thought I'd never see you again.

NURSE. Me either.

DOCTOR X. You're all I think about. Day and night. Afternoon. Morning. When I'm dreaming. When I'm awake. When I'm washing the dishes or loading my syringe. When I'm thinking about getting a cat, really I'm thinking about you. I do it all for you.

NURSE. I wish you would stop.

DOCTOR X. If I can't have love, no one can.

NURSE. That seems unfair.

DOCTOR X. Tell me — What is your name?

NURSE. You don't know?

DOCTOR X. No.

NURSE. Well, let's keep it this way.

DOCTOR X. Why is it I can't remember your name, yet all I think of is you?

44

NURSE. Maybe it's because I hit you on the head.

DOCTOR X. You did?

NURSE. Before I left.

DOCTOR X. Oh.

NURSE. You were sleeping so peacefully. I wrote the note and I put it where I thought you would see it.

DOCTOR X. You didn't sign it.

NURSE. I thought it was a very polite note but I thought maybe you didn't necessarily understand polite based on my past experiences with you. So I hit you over the head with a frying pan just to be sure you got the message. You didn't wake up so I hit you again just to be sure. Then I checked your vitals and everything was okay so I went to work. And I never saw you again. Now it turns out you're Doctor X.

DOCTOR X. And you're, Molly?

NURSE. No.

DOCTOR X. Sylvia?

NURSE. No.

DOCTOR X. Gertrude.

NURSE. No.

DOCTOR X. Betsy?

NURSE. Listen, I'm not going to tell you. In fact I'm thinking of hitting you over the head again just to make sure you don't remember that I work here.

DOCTOR X. Why didn't it work out between us?

NURSE. It just didn't.

DOCTOR X. Your face.

NURSE. Please don't say it.

DOCTOR X. It's like a plate.

NURSE. Oh, God.

DOCTOR X. I may be handcuffed to the bed right now, but that won't always be the case. We can run off together. You could even help me escape.

NURSE. I'm going to transfer to a different hospital.

DOCTOR X. Don't do that.

NURSE. I might move to a different state.

DOCTOR X. We could move together.

NURSE. This is the last time you'll see me.

DOCTOR X. You don't know that. No one ever knows that.

NURSE. I'll make sure this time.

DOCTOR X. No.

NURSE. It was good to see you. I think I had to see you. I had to know. Now I know I made the right decision.

DOCTOR X. No!

NURSE. Goodbye Doctor X.

DOCTOR X. Nooooo! *(Nurse exits.)* Noooo! Come back! Come back.

21

In another part of the hospital, Peter and Lisa.

LISA. You're afraid of me now.

PETER. No.

LISA. Yes, you are. You see now another part of me you didn't know was there and you thought you knew me and now you don't know what you know. Maybe so many facets of a human being frighten you or maybe now you are afraid for my safety or for your own. You think that you will never be able to sleep if I'm not in bed with you because you are worried I will be putting myself in danger somewhere — that I may be tied to a chair above a boiling vat in some lair or dangling from a wire three hundred feet off the ground.

PETER. Oh.

LISA. What?

PETER. I hadn't thought of that until you said something.

LISA. Can you adapt to a relationship in which one of us is a Crimefighter?

PETER. Um —

LISA. I'm asking this terrified. I'm standing here terrified again.

PETER. You lied to me.

LISA. No. No! Well, sort of.

PETER. Is there anything else you're hiding from me?

LISA. I don't think so. How about you?

PETER. No.

LISA. You're hiding your heart. *(Pause.)*

PETER. Maybe.

LISA. You're building a wall around it or a candy shell. You're afraid I might just eat it.

PETER. I have concerns.

LISA. I have a feeling in the pit of my stomach like right before you rejected me the first time. Are you about to give me my walking papers?

PETER. Oh, Lisa!

LISA. Yes?

PETER. I need to think!! *(Peter exits, upset.)*

22

In front of Doctor X's hospital room. Nina enters to relieve Sally.

NINA. I'll take over.

SALLY. Are you sure?

NINA. You're tired. It's been a long shift.

SALLY. Are you rested?

NINA. I went home and lied in the bed. I may not have closed my eyes, but I rested.

SALLY. You couldn't sleep.

NINA. No.

SALLY. Too excited.

NINA. Yes.

SALLY. You sure you can handle this?

NINA. Of course. I've done this a thousand times.

SALLY. But this time —

NINA. What?

SALLY. Nothing.

NINA. Go. Go. Get some rest.

SALLY. Okay, then. Okay. Okay. Bye, then. Okay. Be careful.

NINA. I'm always careful. *(Sally looks back one more time then exits.)*

23

Peter in his workshop in the hospital, takes an artificial heart out of a box. It beats.

PETER. Here you are, my spare heart. Mother said, always have a spare. You never know, she said. Do everything twice. Just in case. Always have an extra pencil. Always bring an extra sandwich. And give it away if you can. To the kid with the torn jacket who smells like pee. And if they say "thank you," say "you're welcome" or "think nothing of it" or "no thanks is necessary." Tell them, "I can see you're a human being who needs something. We all need something sometimes and if I can be the one to help, well that is good, but next time it could be you that helps and that will be good too." Always do what you can to help. And if you think someone is laughing at you, look away. Look away. You'll save them all some day, she said. And now I will. I look to you, artificial heart. I look to you and I hope you know how to beat endlessly like I taught you. Because I'm going to make a million of you, and then another million, and another. Anyone who wants you, can have you. Anyone who feels weak will be made strong by your comforting weight and your life-saving pumping. You will be the circulatory saver of this world. But right now, I'm the one in need of your help. I'm the weak one, the sick, the damaged, the other. I'm the kid with the torn jacket, except the jacket is a heart. Tomorrow, they will crack my chest open and put you inside, and then I will never need to be afraid again.

24

Nina stands in the room of Doctor X. She stares at him. He does not seem to notice.

DOCTOR X. Right there. Could almost touch her. Face like a plate.

NINA. Um …

DOCTOR X. She'll regret it. I'll make her regret it.

NINA. Doctor X?

DOCTOR X. What? What do you want? It's not enough to hand-cuff me to the bed. You've come to jeer at me.

NINA. No. I'm not. I came — I don't know why I came.

DOCTOR X. Well, I don't know why you came.

NINA. I'm sorry. I'll go. *(Nina does not move.)*

DOCTOR X. Go, then.

NINA. I'm sorry. *(Nina starts to leave.)*

DOCTOR X. Wait!

NINA. What?!

DOCTOR X. Why were you looking at me like that?

NINA. Like what?

DOCTOR X. There. You're doing it again.

NINA. No, I'm not.

DOCTOR X. I don't think anyone has ever looked at me like that before. It's so familiar yet — no, I can't place it … no, wait. I know! I've had this expression myself. I've seen it on my face when I've accidentally caught my reflection in silverware or drugstore windows. I know this expression. Oh, I know it.

NINA. You do? Well, I guess I — It's embarrassing. Please, look away.

DOCTOR X. I can't.

NINA. Please. Try to understand. I don't mean to look like this but when I see you, I guess I lose control over any thought of control of my face or body or demeanor. Just being here with you …

DOCTOR X. I understand.

NINA. You do?

49

DOCTOR X. You'd be surprised how understanding I can be.

NINA. I wish that were true.

DOCTOR X. *(Scary aggressive.)* I am understanding!

NINA. Oh. You're so forceful.

DOCTOR X. Yeah?

NINA. Wow.

DOCTOR X. Huh. Okay. Well then. Okay.

NINA. Yes.

DOCTOR X. Okay.

NINA. It's too bad you're evil.

DOCTOR X. I'm not evil.

NINA. Well. Anyway.

DOCTOR X. Sometimes things don't turn out the way we think they will. You know?

NINA. Yeah.

DOCTOR X. Perhaps you grew up with an idea of what kind of a man you should date and this came from your mom and the TV and magazines and other little girls. But sometimes what you have told yourself you want and what you actually want are not the same things. Sometimes your body and your mind don't agree and you should look at that. And not bandy about words like good and evil which everyone knows don't mean anything anyway when it comes down to it.

NINA. I guess.

DOCTOR X. Think about it.

NINA. I'm thinking.

DOCTOR X. I'm thinking about your body pressed against mine.

NINA. You are?

DOCTOR X. I'm thinking about taking off all your clothes piece by piece.

NINA. Stop!

DOCTOR X. Maybe I'd cut them off you.

NINA. You would?

DOCTOR X. Then I would tear into you, with my hands and my teeth. I would leave marks.

NINA. You would?

DOCTOR X. But that's just what I'm thinking of.

NINA. Oh.

DOCTOR X. I'm harmless.

NINA. You are?

DOCTOR X. It's just that my heart is so big. I just try to help everyone.

NINA. You do?

DOCTOR X. It may not seem like help to you, but we just have different perspectives.

NINA. I know.

DOCTOR X. I'd like to help you right now.

NINA. You would?

DOCTOR X. You need attention.

NINA. I know.

DOCTOR X. I'd like to hold you.

NINA. You — what?

DOCTOR X. I want to hold you. Can I hold you?

NINA. Yes! *(Nina goes to him. He tries to hold her.)*

DOCTOR X. Darnit. These darn handcuffs. You don't have the key, do you?

NINA. Oh, no. I shouldn't.

DOCTOR X. I just want to hold you. That's all.

NINA. That's all?

DOCTOR X. Just for a second.

NINA. Well, I guess if it's only for a second. *(She undoes one of his handcuffs.)*

DOCTOR X. The other one too.

NINA. Okay, don't try anything.

DOCTOR X. I wouldn't dream of it. *(The other is undone and he wraps his arms around her. He kisses her deeply. While doing this, he takes the keys from her hand and tosses them across the room. Then he handcuffs her arms to the bed, removes her wristband.)*

NINA. What's that?

DOCTOR X. What? *(Doctor X kisses her again, long and hard. Then he climbs out of bed.)*

NINA. Hey, wait.

DOCTOR X. I won't forget you. Probably.

NINA. Where are you going?

DOCTOR X. I have unfinished business.

NINA. But what about us?

DOCTOR X. Sorry. *(Doctor X leaves. Nina sobs.)*

25

Time has passed. Sally and Jazmin are in Doctor X's room with Nina.

NINA. He just left and I let him. He tricked me and I let it happen.

SALLY. I blame myself.

JAZMIN. So do I.

SALLY. I saw the weakness in you. The confusion, but I let you guard him anyway.

NINA. I let you down.

SALLY. No.

JAZMIN. No.

SALLY. You're only human. I underestimated the pull of the heart.

NINA. Still, I was a fool.

SALLY. Enough of that now. Now, we go find him. He's out there somewhere, as dangerous as ever, more dangerous maybe because now he can't be killed by his own poison. We need to leave now while there is still a trail.

NINA. There's something else.

JAZMIN. What?

NINA. He is in love. It's the cause of his madness. Now that we have his fingerprints, his DNA, his real name, we can research his past and find the woman he loves. We find her, we find him.

SALLY. Good work. You stay here and get to work on that. Jazmin and I will hit the streets. *(Jazmin and Sally exit in a hurry.)*

26

A restaurant. Lisa sits at a table. Peter approaches.

PETER. You came.

LISA. Yes. *(Peter sits.)*

PETER. I'm sorry I ran off like that.

LISA. It's okay. I mean, I accept your apology.

PETER. There's something I should tell you. Tomorrow, I'm scheduled for surgery. I mean, surgery on me. To put my spare heart in.

LISA. So soon.

PETER. Yes. I know you don't want me to, but —

LISA. No. I know it's necessary. Sometimes necessary things must happen.

PETER. Yes.

LISA. You know, all this time, my heart has been like a fist, pounding, knocking people around. But I never meant it to be like that. And I'm aware of the damage behind me. I can look back and see it. And I'm sorry for it all. But I feel the pull again and I know my heart wants me to run as fast as I can. It wants to protect me. I've always listened to it before.

PETER. You're going to run?

LISA. I'm trying not to.

PETER. I want to tell you. Before I go under the knife. I love you.

LISA. You do?

PETER. Yes. So I don't know if that will make you run all the faster, but there it is out there. My heart on a plate. Take it and eat it. Soon, I'll have a new one. *(Sally and Jazmin enter.)*

SALLY. Lisa. Sorry to interrupt.

JAZMIN. Sorry. Hi.

SALLY. We believe Doctor X is still in the city. We're organizing a city-wide search immediately. *(Lisa looks at Peter.)*

PETER. Go.

LISA. You sure?

PETER. I'll worry about you, you'll worry about me. And maybe when I wake, you'll be there. Won't you? *(Lisa leaves with the Crimefighters, possibly dramatically, possibly not.)*

27

Peter is on a gurney. Nurse is talking to him while wheeling him into surgery.

NURSE. I wanted to get in on your surgery, you know, so you'd have a friend there. But Clarice is doing it instead.
PETER. That's okay.
NURSE. Yeah, I'm sure it will be fine. Clarice is really good.
PETER. I know.
NURSE. I asked if I could bring you in here though.
PETER. Thanks.
NURSE. No problem. My pleasure. You're very brave.
PETER. Oh, no. Not me.
NURSE. The anesthesiologist will be in in a second. You want me to wait?
PETER. No, that's okay.
NURSE. I could hold your hand.
PETER. No, I'm fine.
NURSE. Where's, uh, your girlfriend. She couldn't make it?
PETER. She had to work.
NURSE. Oh, well, I guess when you have to work ... Listen, I might not be here when you wake up.
PETER. Oh, that's okay.
NURSE. No, I mean, I'm not going to work here anymore.
PETER. Oh, I'm sorry to hear that.
NURSE. Are you?
PETER. What?
NURSE. I really enjoyed working with you, a lot. But my ex-boyfriend is back and it's not safe for me here. I feel stupid even saying it, but you know, he's killed people.
PETER. I'm sorry to hear that. You'll be missed.
NURSE. Really? Thanks. *(Nurse turns to go and then returns.)* Say,

54

since we may not see each other ever again, I was just wondering ... could I have a kiss goodbye? *(Peter gestures for her to come closer. She bends over him. He kisses her on the cheek.)* Oh. Thanks. *(Exit Nurse.)*

28

Peter awakes to find himself strapped to the bed. There is a figure nearby in the dark.

PETER. I can't move. My arms! Nurse! *(Doctor X moves into the light.)*

DOCTOR X. Shhhh. Quiet now. I don't want any trouble.

PETER. You! But — how?

DOCTOR X. I've been hiding in the ceiling, crawling from room to room looking for you. When I found you, I killed the doctor and nurse who were about to operate on you and then I woke you up.

PETER. But why?

DOCTOR X. You operated on me. Now I'll operate on you. I tried to kill myself and you brought me back. You probably should have let me die. But now, I'm here and you're here and I owe you something. *(Peter tries to shout out but Doctor X puts the mask over his nose and mouth and soon, Peter is unconscious.)* There now, that's better. It's so hard to talk to people when they can talk back. *(The lights change.)* They say it's like riding a bicycle, you never forget how to perform surgery. But I'm not sure they were talking about those of us with brain damage. We'll have to see, just have to see. My hand seems to know what to do. Sometimes the hand knows things the brain doesn't and we should just trust the hand. Now we make the incision. How about there? That seems to be a good place for a heart. I don't have to think when I'm working. I can just slide into the moment, escape into the process. Surgery is a kind of escapism. You can leave your self behind and cut cut cut. It makes me wonder if my self is still here. Maybe I was never lost. Maybe I was always here, just waiting to pick up a scalpel. It feels good. I'll say that. It feels good. Sleep, now, sleep. I owe you that.

29

The nurses' station. Sally is there dressed as a Crimefighter. Enter Nina dressed as a nurse.

NINA. The trail was cold.

SALLY. I know. He's probably long gone by now. On some island in the Pacific or in Cancun or Kansas.

NINA. Listen, about before...

SALLY. Forget it. We're all human. Let's concentrate on Doctor X's background check. We'll interview the people that knew him. Somewhere in his past is the woman he loved. We find her, we find him. Oh, sorry.

NINA. For what?

SALLY. Nothing. Well, I'll call in Jazmin and tell her to call off the search. *(Sally picks up a phone to call Jazmin. Enter Nurse. She talks to Nina.)*

NURSE. Hi, I just wanted to say thank you. For everything.

SALLY. *(On phone.)* Yeah, that's fine. Just come in.

NINA. We'll miss you.

NURSE. I'll miss you, too. I never could have kicked that dough-nut habit without you.

NINA. It was nothing. Why are you going again? New job?

SALLY. Uh-huh.

NURSE. Well, that's what I've been saying. But ... well, I guess I can tell you the truth. I'm running away from Doctor X.

SALLY. No.

NINA. You don't need to do that.

NURSE. I do actually. He's killing people because of me. The guilt tears me apart, but I told him to stop. What more can I do?

NINA. Why do you think he's killing people because of you?

NURSE. Because that's what he told me. We sort of used to date. You know, before he became Doctor X.

SALLY. I'll call you back.

NINA. You think he might be looking for you?

NURSE. I know he is.

SALLY. Well, we've been looking for you.

NURSE. What do you mean?

SALLY. You can't go. We need your help. *(Lisa enters to hear this last part.)*

NURSE. But —

SALLY. Listen, you can't just run away all the time when things go wrong. I know that feels like the way to go, but sometimes you have to do the scary thing. *(Lights up on Peter waking up in surgery. Doctor X is climbing a ladder, trying to get back in the ceiling.)*

PETER. You.

DOCTOR X. Oh, good, you lived.

PETER. Nurse! Nurse! I need a nurse! *(Doctor X continues to climb.)*

DOCTOR X. Stop that now. I'll be out of here before you know it.

PETER. Nurse! *(Nina enters.)*

NINA. What can I do for you? Oh. You. *(Before Doctor X can get into the ceiling, Nina grabs the ladder and pushes it over. Doctor X falls to the ground.)* You're not getting away this time. *(Nina presses the homing device on her wrist. She and Doctor X begin to fight. At the nurses' station, Lisa, Sally and Jazmin see their wrist contraptions beep and glow red.)*

SALLY. Dr. X! He's here! *(Lisa and Jazmin run to the room and join the fight.)* Please. We need you.

NURSE. But I'm afraid.

SALLY. Fear cannot rule our lives. This is too important. *(Sally runs to join the fight. Nurse stands there while the fight rages in the other room. Finally Nurse makes a decision. She enters the room. When Doctor X sees Nurse he pauses, stops fighting.)*

DOCTOR X. You. *(The Crimefighters pounce on him. And restrain him.)* You stayed.

NURSE. I did.

DOCTOR X. Are you going to come back to me?

NURSE. I'm afraid not. *(The Crimefighters take him away. Nurse looks at Peter longingly and then follows them out.)*

PETER. You stayed.

LISA. I packed my things. I was ready to take off. I was going to go for good. But I couldn't do it. My heart wouldn't let me. It has competing ideas about you.

PETER. I'm grateful to it.

LISA. What about you? Do you still love me with your new heart?

PETER. Of course.

LISA. It doesn't mean it can't be broken.

PETER. You're not going to break it now, are you?

LISA. I'll try not to. Life is unpredictable. There are forces set against our happiness. Things could happen at any time. One of us could die. When I'm out fighting crime. When you cross the street. You could wake up one day and not love me.

PETER. No!

LISA. We'll have to be brave in the face of the unknown. *(Lisa tries to be brave.)* I love you.

PETER. You do?

LISA. That's what my heart is saying.

PETER. Mine, too. *(They kiss.)*

30

Lights up on Doctor X in jail. Peter and Lisa remain on stage.

DOCTOR X. I can feel my insides crawling around like a bowlful of worms. My foreign heart beating in perfectly timed beats. I might be in here, incarcerated, in misery, but you can't keep me long. I have a mission. I have a — I can't remember. All I can see is your face. It's nothing but suffering living like this. Everyone should suffer. No one should be happy. One of these days. I'll get you! I'll get you all! *(Peter and Lisa kiss.)*

End of Play

PROPERTY LIST

2 stethoscopes
Doctor's lab coat
Doctor's bag
Hospital bed
Yellow crime-scene tape
Hypodermic needles
4 crimefighter masks
2 dummies
Business card
Men's hat
Restaurant table and chairs
Men's coat
Artificial heart and box
Screwdriver
Bed sheets and covers
Cell phone
Weapons: swords, nunchakus, etc.
4 wristwatch gadgets/homing devices
Rubber gloves
Medical file
Sink and dishes
Sandwich
Kitchen utensils (various)
Medication on a tray
Doughnuts
Handcuffs and keys
Gurney
Straps to tie a patient down to a bed
Hospital mask for anesthesia
Ladder

SOUND EFFECTS

Flashbulbs, photos being taken
Static from walkie-talkie
Snoring
Beating heart
Men's whistles/catcalls
Car screeching, car crash, car alarms
Men walking into street posts and mailboxes
Huge crash
Normal city noises
Wristwatch gadget beeps
Music
Helicopter

NEW PLAYS

★ **MOTHERHOOD OUT LOUD by Leslie Ayvazian, Brooke Berman, David Cale, Jessica Goldberg, Beth Henley, Lameece Issaq, Claire LaZebnik, Lisa Loomer, Michele Lowe, Marco Pennette, Theresa Rebeck, Luanne Rice, Annie Weisman and Cheryl L. West, conceived by Susan R. Rose and Joan Stein.** When entrusting the subject of motherhood to such a dazzling collection of celebrated American writers, what results is a joyous, moving, hilarious, and altogether thrilling theatrical event. "Never fails to strike both the funny bone and the heart." *—BackStage.* "Packed with wisdom, laughter, and plenty of wry surprises." *—TheaterMania.* [1M, 3W] ISBN: 978-0-8222-2589-8

★ **COCK by Mike Bartlett.** When John takes a break from his boyfriend, he accidentally meets the girl of his dreams. Filled with guilt and indecision, he decides there is only one way to straighten this out. "[A] brilliant and blackly hilarious feat of provocation." *—Independent.* "A smart, prickly and rewarding view of sexual and emotional confusion." *—Evening Standard.* [3M, 1W] ISBN: 978-0-8222-2766-3

★ **F. Scott Fitzgerald's THE GREAT GATSBY adapted for the stage by Simon Levy.** Jay Gatsby, a self-made millionaire, passionately pursues the elusive Daisy Buchanan. Nick Carraway, a young newcomer to Long Island, is drawn into their world of obsession, greed and danger. "Levy's combination of narration, dialogue and action delivers most of what is best in the novel." *—Seattle Post-Intelligencer.* "A beautifully crafted interpretation of the 1925 novel which defined the Jazz Age." *—London Free Press.* [5M, 4W] ISBN: 978-0-8222-2727-4

★ **LONELY, I'M NOT by Paul Weitz.** At an age when most people are discovering what they want to do with their lives, Porter has been married and divorced, earned seven figures as a corporate "ninja," and had a nervous breakdown. It's been four years since he's had a job or a date, and he's decided to give life another shot. "Critic's pick!" *—NY Times.* "An enjoyable ride." *—NY Daily News.* [3M, 3W] ISBN: 978-0-8222-2734-2

★ **ASUNCION by Jesse Eisenberg.** Edgar and Vinny are not racist. In fact, Edgar maintains a blog condemning American imperialism, and Vinny is three-quarters into a Ph.D. in Black Studies. When Asuncion becomes their new roommate, the boys have a perfect opportunity to demonstrate how open-minded they truly are. "Mr. Eisenberg writes lively dialogue that strikes plenty of comic sparks." *—NY Times.* "An almost ridiculously enjoyable portrait of slacker trauma among would-be intellectuals." *—Newsday.* [2M, 2W] ISBN: 978-0-8222-2630-7

DRAMATISTS PLAY SERVICE, INC.
440 Park Avenue South, New York, NY 10016 212-683-8960 Fax 212-213-1539
postmaster@dramatists.com www.dramatists.com

NEW PLAYS

★ **THE PICTURE OF DORIAN GRAY by Roberto Aguirre-Sacasa, based on the novel by Oscar Wilde.** Preternaturally handsome Dorian Gray has his portrait painted by his college classmate Basil Hallwood. When their mutual friend Henry Wotton offers to include it in a show, Dorian makes a fateful wish—that his portrait should grow old instead of him—and strikes an unspeakable bargain with the devil. [5M, 2W] ISBN: 978-0-8222-2590-4

★ **THE LYONS by Nicky Silver.** As Ben Lyons lies dying, it becomes clear that he and his wife have been at war for many years, and his impending demise has brought no relief. When they're joined by their children all efforts at a sentimental goodbye to the dying patriarch are soon abandoned. "Hilariously frank, clear-sighted, compassionate and forgiving." *–NY Times.* "Mordant, dark and rich." *–Associated Press.* [3M, 3W] ISBN: 978-0-8222-2659-8

★ **STANDING ON CEREMONY by Mo Gaffney, Jordan Harrison, Moisés Kaufman, Neil LaBute, Wendy MacLeod, José Rivera, Paul Rudnick, and Doug Wright, conceived by Brian Shnipper.** Witty, warm and occasionally wacky, these plays are vows to the blessings of equality, the universal challenges of relationships and the often hilarious power of love. "CEREMONY puts a human face on a hot-button issue and delivers laughter and tears rather than propaganda." *–BackStage.* [3M, 3W] ISBN: 978-0-8222-2654-3

★ **ONE ARM by Moisés Kaufman, based on the short story and screenplay by Tennessee Williams.** Ollie joins the Navy and becomes the lightweight boxing champion of the Pacific Fleet. Soon after, he loses his arm in a car accident, and he turns to hustling to survive. "[A] fast, fierce, brutally beautiful stage adaptation." *–NY Magazine.* "A fascinatingly lurid, provocative and fatalistic piece of theater." *–Variety.* [7M, 1W] ISBN: 978-0-8222-2564-5

★ **AN ILIAD by Lisa Peterson and Denis O'Hare.** A modern-day retelling of Homer's classic. Poetry and humor, the ancient tale of the Trojan War and the modern world collide in this captivating theatrical experience. "Shocking, glorious, primal and deeply satisfying." *–Time Out NY.* "Explosive, altogether breathtaking." *–Chicago Sun-Times.* [1M] ISBN: 978-0-8222-2687-1

★ **THE COLUMNIST by David Auburn.** At the height of the Cold War, Joe Alsop is the nation's most influential journalist, beloved, feared and courted by the Washington world. But as the '60s dawn and America undergoes dizzying change, the intense political dramas Joe is embroiled in become deeply personal as well. "Intensely satisfying." *–Bloomberg News.* [5M, 2W] ISBN: 978-0-8222-2699-4

DRAMATISTS PLAY SERVICE, INC.
440 Park Avenue South, New York, NY 10016 212-683-8960 Fax 212-213-1539
postmaster@dramatists.com   www.dramatists.com

NEW PLAYS

★ **BENGAL TIGER AT THE BAGHDAD ZOO by Rajiv Joseph.** The lives of two American Marines and an Iraqi translator are forever changed by an encounter with a quick-witted tiger who haunts the streets of war-torn Baghdad. "[A] boldly imagined, harrowing and surprisingly funny drama." –*NY Times*. "Tragic yet darkly comic and highly imaginative." –*CurtainUp*. [5M, 2W] ISBN: 978-0-8222-2565-2

★ **THE PITMEN PAINTERS by Lee Hall, inspired by a book by William Feaver.** Based on the triumphant true story, a group of British miners discover a new way to express themselves and unexpectedly become art-world sensations. "Excitingly ambiguous, in-the-moment theater." –*NY Times*. "Heartfelt, moving and deeply politicized." –*Chicago Tribune*. [5M, 2W] ISBN: 978-0-8222-2507-2

★ **RELATIVELY SPEAKING by Ethan Coen, Elaine May and Woody Allen.** In TALKING CURE, Ethan Coen uncovers the sort of insanity that can only come from family. Elaine May explores the hilarity of passing in GEORGE IS DEAD. In HONEYMOON MOTEL, Woody Allen invites you to the sort of wedding day you won't forget. "Firecracker funny." –*NY Times*. "A rollicking good time." –*New Yorker*. [8M, 7W] ISBN: 978-0-8222-2394-8

★ **SONS OF THE PROPHET by Stephen Karam.** If to live is to suffer, then Joseph Douaihy is more alive than most. With unexplained chronic pain and the fate of his reeling family on his shoulders, Joseph's health, sanity, and insurance premium are on the line. "Explosively funny." –*NY Times*. "At once deep, deft and beautifully made." –*New Yorker*. [5M, 3W] ISBN: 978-0-8222-2597-3

★ **THE MOUNTAINTOP by Katori Hall.** A gripping reimagination of events the night before the assassination of the civil rights leader Dr. Martin Luther King, Jr. "An ominous electricity crackles through the opening moments." –*NY Times*. "[A] thrilling, wild, provocative flight of magical realism." –*Associated Press*. "Crackles with theatricality and a humanity more moving than sainthood." –*NY Newsday*. [1M, 1W] ISBN: 978-0-8222-2603-1

★ **ALL NEW PEOPLE by Zach Braff.** Charlie is 35, heartbroken, and just wants some time away from the rest of the world. Long Beach Island seems to be the perfect escape until his solitude is interrupted by a motley parade of misfits who show up and change his plans. "Consistently and sometimes sensationally funny." –*NY Times*. "A morbidly funny play about the trendy new existential condition of being young, adorable, and miserable." –*Variety*. [2M, 2W] ISBN: 978-0-8222-2562-1

DRAMATISTS PLAY SERVICE, INC.
440 Park Avenue South, New York, NY 10016 212-683-8960 Fax 212-213-1539
postmaster@dramatists.com www.dramatists.com

NEW PLAYS

★ **CLYBOURNE PARK by Bruce Norris.** WINNER OF THE 2011 PULITZER PRIZE AND 2012 TONY AWARD. Act One takes place in 1959 as community leaders try to stop the sale of a home to a black family. Act Two is set in the same house in the present day as the now predominantly African-American neighborhood battles to hold its ground. "Vital, sharp-witted and ferociously smart." –*NY Times.* "A theatrical treasure…Indisputably, uproariously funny." –*Entertainment Weekly.* [4M, 3W] ISBN: 978-0-8222-2697-0

★ **WATER BY THE SPOONFUL by Quiara Alegría Hudes.** WINNER OF THE 2012 PULITZER PRIZE. A Puerto Rican veteran is surrounded by the North Philadelphia demons he tried to escape in the service. "This is a very funny, warm, and yes uplifting play." –*Hartford Courant.* "The play is a combination poem, prayer and app on how to cope in an age of uncertainty, speed and chaos." –*Variety.* [4M, 3W] ISBN: 978-0-8222-2716-8

★ **RED by John Logan.** WINNER OF THE 2010 TONY AWARD. Mark Rothko has just landed the biggest commission in the history of modern art. But when his young assistant, Ken, gains the confidence to challenge him, Rothko faces the agonizing possibility that his crowning achievement could also become his undoing. "Intense and exciting." –*NY Times.* "Smart, eloquent entertainment." –*New Yorker.* [2M] ISBN: 978-0-8222-2483-9

★ **VENUS IN FUR by David Ives.** Thomas, a beleaguered playwright/director, is desperate to find an actress to play Vanda, the female lead in his adaptation of the classic sadomasochistic tale *Venus in Fur.* "Ninety minutes of good, kinky fun." –*NY Times.* "A fast-paced journey into one man's entrapment by a clever, vengeful female." –*Associated Press.* [1M, 1W] ISBN: 978-0-8222-2603-1

★ **OTHER DESERT CITIES by Jon Robin Baitz.** Brooke returns home to Palm Springs after a six-year absence and announces that she is about to publish a memoir dredging up a pivotal and tragic event in the family's history—a wound they don't want reopened. "Leaves you feeling both moved and gratifyingly sated." –*NY Times.* "A genuine pleasure." –*NY Post.* [2M, 3W] ISBN: 978-0-8222-2605-5

★ **TRIBES by Nina Raine.** Billy was born deaf into a hearing family and adapts brilliantly to his family's unconventional ways, but it's not until he meets Sylvia, a young woman on the brink of deafness, that he finally understands what it means to be understood. "A smart, lively play." –*NY Times.* "[A] bright and boldly provocative drama." –*Associated Press.* [3M, 2W] ISBN: 978-0-8222-2751-9

DRAMATISTS PLAY SERVICE, INC.
440 Park Avenue South, New York, NY 10016 212-683-8960 Fax 212-213-1539
postmaster@dramatists.com   www.dramatists.com